AF598736

LOCKHEED CONSTELLATION

A Legends of Flight Illustrated History

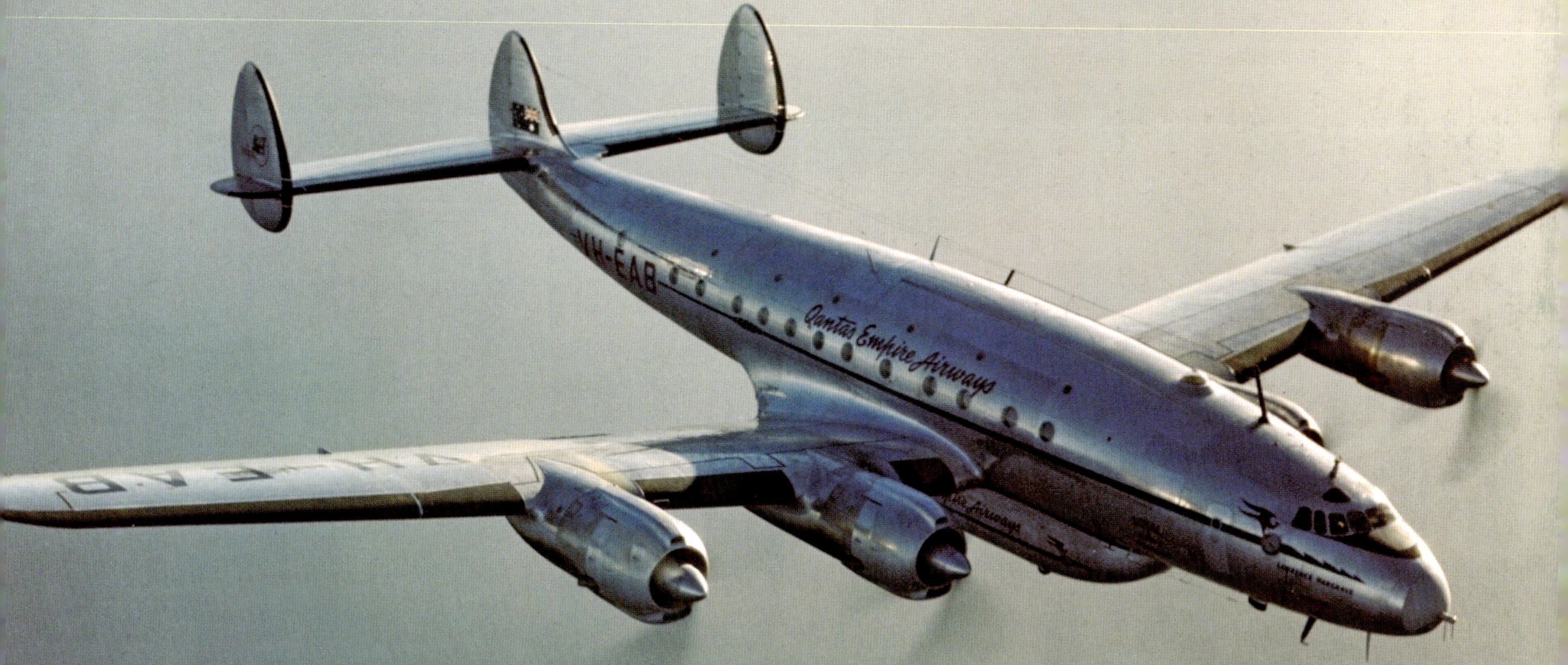

WOLFGANG BORGMANN

Other Schiffer books by the author

Douglas DC-4, DC-6, and DC-7: A Legends of Flight Illustrated History, 978-0-7643-6648-2

S.E. 210 Caravelle: A Legends of Flight Illustrated History, 978-0-7643-6650-5

Douglas DC-9: A Legends of Flight Illustrated History, 978-0-7643-6484-6

Library of Congress Control Number: 2024931526

Type set in Minion/DIN/Axia

ISBN: 978-0-7643-6822-6
Printed in India

Published by Schiffer Publishing, Ltd.
4880 Lower Valley Road
Atglen, PA 19310
Phone: (610) 593-1777; Fax: (610) 593-2002
Email: Info@schifferbooks.com
Web: www.schifferbooks.com

Dedicated

To Mila

CONTENTS

INTRODUCTION

This book takes you on an imaginary journey back in time to the 1950s—that era of air travel commonly referred to as the "Golden Age of Aviation." An irretrievable time when flying was an elite, extremely expensive means of transportation for the lucky few. Thanks to a cartel set up by the global airline association IATA, which dictated airfares for all airlines, the only way they could compete with one another was by offering outstanding service. And they did so in a way unimaginable today, in the form of "pure luxury"!

On a warm and clear summer night in 1955, if you looked up at the sky and admired the constellations, you might be lucky enough to hear the hum and see the blurred navigation lights of one of those majestic silver birds flying slowly across the sky on its way to its unknown destination. And with a little imagination, these lights seemed to resemble beautiful comets and constellations. No wonder Lockheed chose the poetic name Constellation for what many aviation fans consider to be the most beautiful commercial airliner ever built.

Famous entertainment figures, self-made millionaires, and honeymooners transformed the cabins of these Constellations and Super Constellations and the Starliner into mystical, romantic places. Looked after by the cabin crew with the highest level of service and comfort, it was the ultimate form of luxury travel in this truly "golden" age. But this did not limit the Constellation's fields of operation. Just as important was its military use as a troop transport and reconnaissance aircraft—and even as the US "Air Force One" presidential aircraft. This book also gives this spectrum of use the space it deserves.

Mona Lisa of the Skies, or Queen of the Skies—even with such flowery phrases, admirers of the Lockheed Constellation find it difficult to put their enthusiasm for this legendary propeller-driven airliner into words. But what is so special about this aircraft type, which even many decades after production ended in Burbank, California, still makes the hearts of those around the globe infected by the aviation virus beat faster?

Since its maiden flight in January 1943, the Connie has fascinated its fan club. In those eight decades, commercial aircraft capable of flying faster, higher, and farther, some perhaps even more beautiful, have left the final-assembly lines of aircraft manufacturers. But who can resist the fascination of a Lockheed Constellation at the sight of its curved dolphin-shaped fuselage, its three-part tail, its long-legged landing gear, the aluminum panels of its outer skin trimmed to aerodynamic perfection?

The queen of the skies in all her beauty. *Lockheed Martin*

You can't get more symbolic than that. This historic model shows the queen of the skies being accompanied through the skies by a Lockheed Constellation. *Author's collection*

Its nimbus is certainly also due to the colorful people who helped give birth to it in the early days. First and foremost was the first American billionaire, business tycoon, oil magnate, movie mogul, pilot, airline owner, and very eccentric aviator Howard Hughes. Or the legendary Lockheed chief designer Kelly Johnson, whose design signature can be found not only in the Constellation, but also in the legendary designs from the "Skunk Works," such as the U-2 spy plane or the SR-71, which flew three times faster than sound.

But what would the flying legends be without those airlines whose famous names they carried around the world? Such as Pan American World Airways (PAA), for example, or Transcontinental & Western Air, which called itself Trans World Airlines (TWA) from 1950 onward, which, as launch customers, are inextricably linked with the history of the Lockheed Constellation. With their Connies, they opened the trade routes of the modern era at a leisurely propeller pace after the end of World War II, those global routes on which the daily flow of goods, like the arteries of world trade, span our globe today. We have long taken it for granted that an item ordered online will fly around the globe to be delivered to our doorstep by the parcel carrier. It is a service that was first made possible by air freight, which was codeveloped on a large scale by Constellation operators such as Flying Tiger Lines and Seaboard & Western. But former L-749, L-1049, and L-1649A passenger planes of various airlines converted to freighters by Lockheed Aircraft Service Inc. also contributed to the rapid increase in air freight volume.

Those who trade and make friends do not wage war against each other, a simple realization that was largely fueled by the fleets of Constellations operated by international airlines around the globe in the pioneering years of air travel.

The development of those travel routes for goods and people was due to the foresight of visionaries such as Howard Hughes and Pan American Airways founder and president Juan T. Trippe, who brought the world a little closer together with their Constellations. When, at the end of World War II, PAA and TWA were finally able to take delivery of their Lockheed L-049s, ordered in prewar days, they immediately deployed the aircraft on their global route networks. The Connies, equipped with a pressurized cabin, flew at an

Trans World Airlines was involved in the development of the Lockheed Constellation like no other airline. *John Bezosky, collections and restoration manager, Pima Air and Space Museum*

altitude of around 20,000 feet (6,000 meters [m]) and, for example, covered the route from New York to Lisbon, Portugal, including refueling stops, in around ten hours. Thus, 1946 soon became a record year for PAA—with more than 1,100 Atlantic crossings by its Lockheed L-049 fleet, which shuttled between its hub in New York and destinations in London, Shannon, Vienna, Bermuda, and what was then the Belgian Congo in Africa.

On the initiative of PAA as well as other American airlines, the global airline association—IATA—approved the introduction of a cheaper "tourist class" on transatlantic routes in 1951. It premiered in May 1952 with great success. While most people traveled by ocean liner between Europe and the United States until the mid-1950s, more passengers crossed the North Atlantic by air for the first time in 1957 thanks to this cheaper tourist class fare—many of them aboard a four-engine Lockheed!

Evening atmosphere at Lufthansa's maintenance base at Hamburg in the late 1950s. *Lufthansa*

Admired by visitors to Zurich Airport through the terminal's large panoramic windows: L-049 PP-PDC, operated by Panair do Brasil. *ETH Zurich*

The British airline Skyways of London was one of the many small operators that procured Lockheed Constellations on the secondhand market. It operated four L-749As and one L-149. *bsl-mlh-planes.net / Werner Gysin-Aegerter*

Elegance personified: one of TWA's L-1049Gs with wingtip fuel tanks over the skyline of New York City. *Lockheed Martin*

For many Connie fans, with its longer and thinner redesigned wings, the L-1649A was the ultimate Mona Lisa of the *sky. Lufthansa*

Not only PAA and TWA, but also Air France, the British airline BOAC, El Al of Israel, the Dutch airline KLM, and American Overseas Airlines (AOA) belonged to the exclusive Constellation Club, which flew its first L-049s across the North Atlantic. These relatively spartan aircraft were followed in 1948 by the more comfortable and efficient L-749 Constellations, which were better suited for overseas routes. The further-improved L-749A led to the L-1049 Super Constellation in 1950. The series culminated with the ultimate L-1649A Starliner in 1956. These luxuriously appointed aircraft, named Super Starliner by Air France, Super Star by Lufthansa, and Jetstream by TWA, were the last flicker of the propeller age before the first jets gradually displaced the graceful propeller-driven airliners from the main air traffic routes starting in the fall of 1958. It was an era filled with luxury and adventure, but also numerous air accidents, in which the Lockheed Constellation series unfortunately accounted for a significant share.

In 1998 and 2007, I had the distinct pleasure of flying aboard a Constellation and a Super Constellation as a passenger. Their spartan cabins, which reflected their previous military use, could in no way convey the luxury of early commercial aviation, but on these sightseeing flights, which originated in the northern German Hanseatic city of Hamburg, the experience of flying, rather than comfort, was also paramount. The sound of the radial engines, the sight of their hot exhaust flames, and the propellers turning with a sonorous hum was a pleasure from the first second to the last and unfortunately came to an end far too quickly!

Both aircraft, the L-749 N494TW and the L-1049 HB-RSC were no longer airworthy when this book was first printed. And in the spring of 2024, it was more than doubtful for both aircraft whether this would ever be the case again. This uncertainty as to how long such flight and restoration projects will run, and whether possibly still new flying Connies will be admired in the sky, leads to my principal restriction to the history of the Lockheed Constellation series. The danger of writing about outdated "news" is too great even as this book goes to press. Although I am of course aware that at the time of going to press there was still a Super Constellation flying in Australia, and several Connie and Super Connie restoration projects were taking place in the United States. I was very closely associated with Lufthansa's L-1649A project, which unfortunately failed in the end, for over ten years. For the reasons mentioned above, I prefer to leave reporting on current topics to the colleagues of those trade magazines that write about historic aviation.

Be it the original Constellation, the stretched Super Constellation with its distinctive tip tanks, or the imposing Starliner, the elegant design by Kelly Johnson is an outstanding creation of aircraft design in all its facets: to this day, for me, the only true queen of the skies!

Welcome to this fascinating journey back to a bygone era of aviation and military aviation.

Wolfgang Borgmann
Bielefeld, spring 2024

Most Super Constellation and Starliner customers installed comfortable lounges in the aft fuselages of their aircraft. *Lockheed Martin*

The US Air Force officially took delivery of this RC-121D on March 20, 1956. As of July 1956, it and its sister aircraft were renamed as the EC-121D. *Lockheed Martin*

Servicing an L-749 of South African Airways on the tarmac of the Johannesburg airport. *THL Image Collection / SAR Publicity and Travel Department*

The Australian airline QANTAS was a loyal Lockheed customer and operated Constellations and Super Constellations of various versions. *QANTAS*

Two Lufthansa L-1049Gs flying in formation during a charter flight. *Didi Krauss*

Conscientious preflight checks were already standard practice at Lufthansa in the Connie era. *Lufthansa*

One of two R7V-2s built for the US Navy, which differed from their YC-121F counterparts in the US Air Force primarily in the shape of their wings. Their short wings, designed for speed, were also to be fitted to the civilian L-1249. *Lockheed Martin*

The author of this book had his first personal Connie flight experience in this L-749 in MATS colors. *Lockheed Martin*

Impressions of the Connie flight from Hamburg in 1998. *Author's photos*

Labels like this were distributed by the Constellation Group in the 1990s. *Author's collection*

The author during his flight in the Super Constellation in 2007. *Wolfgang Borgmann*

And this is the subject of the photo being taken by the author in the previous picture.
Wolfgang Borgmann

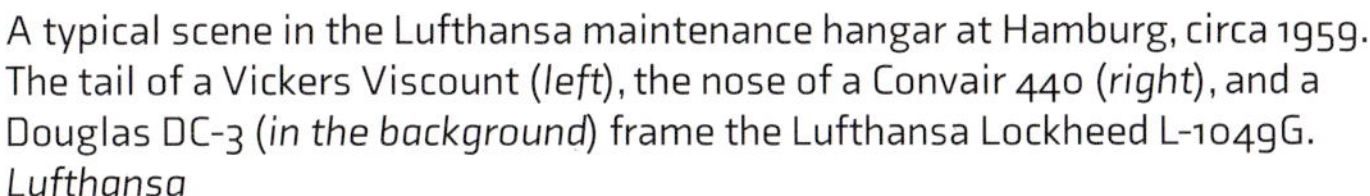

A typical scene in the Lufthansa maintenance hangar at Hamburg, circa 1959. The tail of a Vickers Viscount (*left*), the nose of a Convair 440 (*right*), and a Douglas DC-3 (*in the background*) frame the Lufthansa Lockheed L-1049G.
Lufthansa

These two charming TWA stewardesses wish readers an exciting flight through the fascinating history of the Lockheed Constellation.
Lockheed Martin

The Queen of the North Atlantic. *Lockheed Martin*

CHAPTER 1
HOW IT ALL BEGAN

TOP SECRET

The story of the Lockheed Constellation's creation is closely associated with a handful of names in American aviation history: Howard Hughes, Jack Fry, Bob Gross, and Clarence "Kelly" Johnson. And had the Transcontinental & Western Air board of directors not denied its president, Jack Frye, funding for five Boeing 307 Stratoliners ordered exclusively for the airline in 1939, the Constellation might never have been built. They say that in every bad there is also some good. That included Frye's desperate search for backers to finance the aircraft, which were already in final assembly at Boeing. And fast! Not only because he had given his word to Boeing, but also because TWA desperately needed modern aircraft to equip itself against ever-increasing competition. The Stratoliners, he calculated, would be the first pressurized passenger aircraft to pave TWA's way into the future. In this desperate situation, he contacted Howard Hughes, legendary tycoon and the heir to the Hughes Tool Company. The eccentric, aviation-infatuated, first multi-billionaire in American history seized his opportunity, bought a large part of TWA's shares—and promptly dismissed the entire board of directors. It could not have come at a better time for Jack Frye. The Boeing deal for five Stratoliners was saved—and his TWA remained in the race.

While Howard Hughes came on board at TWA, Robert E. Gross, Walter T. Varney, and Lloyd Stearman acquired the name and sad remains of the unsuccessful Lockheed Company from the bankruptcy trustee for $40,000 on June 6, 1932. Hall L. Hibbard was appointed vice president of the revived aircraft works, while about a year later Clarence L. "Kelly" Johnson joined the small team as aircraft designer. The new team took off with vigor and immediately produced such successful aircraft designs as the Lockheed Model 8 Sirius, Model 10 Electra, and Model 18 Lodestar. What all these aircraft had in common was that they were designed for speed. Floating on a wave of success, Lockheed introduced a four-engine passenger airplane in 1937—the Excalibur. Pan American's Juan T. Trippe showed interest and Lockheed even built a mockup, but development was soon halted. Howard Hughes, enthusiastic about racing airplanes, which he had built at his Hughes Aircraft Company and flew himself, was not unaware of Lockheed's plans for a fast airliner. And so, during a telephone call he asked Jack Frye to make secret contact with Bob Gross. The rest is history.

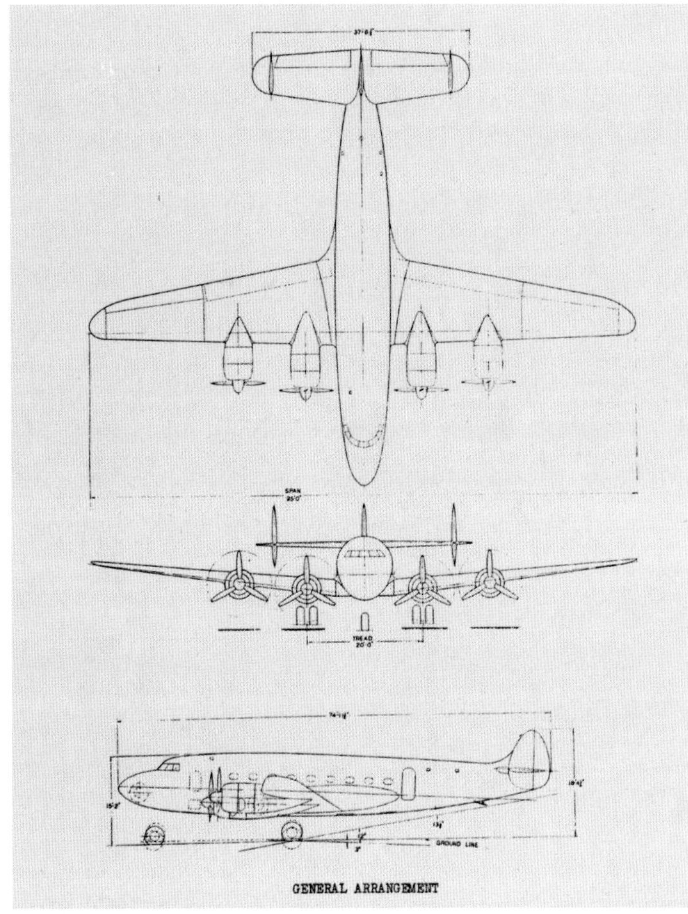

The Excalibur originally planned by Lockheed did not live up to the expectations of the airlines and was abandoned in favor of the Constellation.
Lockheed Martin

CONNIE IN A NUTSHELL

The origins of the Constellation were initially of a purely civilian nature, since multibillionaire aviator Howard Hughes was looking for a very special airliner for his airline Transcontinental & Western Air, in which he had acquired a majority stake in 1938–39. It was to make nonstop transcontinental flights across the United States possible for the first time, flying higher and faster than any other airliner built or planned in the late 1930s. Lockheed Aircraft Works,

The elegant shape of the Constellation was tested in the wind tunnel and aerodynamically refined on the basis of the data obtained there.
Lockheed Martin

which specialized in the design of fast commercial aircraft, seemed the right partner for Hughes to undertake such an ambitious project. Thus, in the first half of 1939, the Lockheed and TWA teams and Howard Hughes sat together in intense secret negotiations that culminated in a contract signed on July 10, 1939, for an initial nine aircraft of the L-49 version designed for TWA. This date is thus considered the Constellation's moment of birth.

The first, again secret, meeting involving Bob Gross, Hall Hibbard, Kelly Johnson, and Howard Hughes took place at the latter's Los Angeles estate. Hughes requested a design that combined speed, range, and passenger comfort. An improved Excalibur was out of the question for him—it had to be a completely new design for his TWA. This initial sounding out was followed by the next secret meeting at the Beverly Hills Hotel in Los Angeles, where concrete matters such as the choice of the right engine were already being discussed. Meeting followed meeting, and again the Beverly Hills Hotel was the scene of the first presentation of Lockheed's design sketches, which were to be given a

Construction of the first Constellation prototype. *Lockheed Martin*

The Constellation prototype, a few steps from its completion. *Lockheed Martin*

name a little later: Constellation. The first studies already showed all the details so unique to the production aircraft: the dolphin-shaped curved fuselage, the triple tail unit, the scaled-up wings of the Lockheed P-38 Lightning, and a speed of 390 miles (630 kilometers [km]) per hour. Faster than any other aircraft of its time! Hughes kept pushing for speed in the countless meetings. Faster, faster, and faster again was his demand on Lockheed. Among the members of the manufacturing team, there was some dispute at first as to whether a cylindrical fuselage shape would not offer advantages in flight, but Kelly Johnson and Bob Gross prevailed. They were so taken with the beauty of the dolphin-shaped fuselage that the in-house critics quickly fell silent. In order to realize these ambitious plans, Lockheed designers focused unconditionally on aerodynamic perfection. The Constellation's drag was a full 13 percent lower than that of the then-competing Douglas DC-4 Skymaster! The curved all-metal fuselage formed an aerodynamically optimal unit with the wings, and the Wright Duplex Cyclone R-3350, with eighteen-cylinder radial engines, had a takeoff power of 2,200 horsepower (hp), twice that of the Boeing

The C-69 prototype after its rollout at Burbank. *Lockheed Martin*

The "aviator" and Constellation initiator Howard Hughes at the controls of one such aircraft. *Author's collection*

The Constellation's chief designer, Clarence L. "Kelly" Johnson (*far left*), was part of this crew during flight testing of the C-69. *Lockheed Martin*

307 Stratoliner. The Lockheed team had already demonstrated with the advanced designs of the Lockheed Vega, Electra, Orion, and Lodestar that they were capable of developing exceptional aircraft far ahead of their time.

Negotiations dragged on, and soon it was time to sign a formal contract between TWA and Lockheed. Howard Hughes, fearing for the secrecy of the project, refused to let anyone else be party to it. Finally, TWA cofounder Tommy Tomlinson came up with the bright idea of assigning his wife, Marge, who worked as a court reporter, to type up the contracts, a suggestion that Howard Hughes also agreed to. Thus, in July 1939, that legendary contract between the Hughes Tool Company, officially acting as buyer, and Lockheed was signed—the Constellation was born! Lockheed had agreed to build the first forty examples of the Model 49 exclusively for TWA at a unit price of $425,000. Lockheed wasn't even allowed to hold sales talks with other airlines until the thirty-fifth aircraft had been delivered to Hughes. This additional agreement was to enable TWA to offer air travel exclusively with the fastest, most comfortable, and farthest-flying passenger aircraft of the time for about two years. Howard Hughes had thus probably pulled off one of the greatest coups in aviation history, because the competition, in particular Pan American Airways president Juan Terry Trippe, was outraged. Only after further negotiations did Hughes allow PAA to purchase forty Constellations of the planned L-149 intercontinental version, since it was not in direct competition with TWA, which at that time operated only on US domestic routes.

SPEED RECORD

It fits the idiosyncratic character of Howard Hughes that the existence of the Constellation project remained secret at his insistence for many months after the contract was signed. Although thousands of employees at Lockheed and TWA were involved with the L-49, not a word leaked out—that alone is an impressive feat. It wasn't until the threat of American involvement in World War II forced Lockheed to disclose all its projects in 1940, under pressure from the US government, that the Constellation was forcibly brought into the public eye.

Production of the Model 49 Constellation began in 1940 with the forty examples for the Hughes Tool Company. Pan American World Airways followed with an order of identical size, split between twenty-two Model 49 aircraft and eighteen Model 149 aircraft planned for intercontinental routes. However, neither TWA nor PAA was to receive their aircraft for the time being.

The reason was the Japanese attack on the American naval base at Pearl Harbor in the Hawaiian Islands on December 7, 1941. Taken completely by surprise by the attack, the United States declared war on Japan just one day later and was thus drawn into the turmoil of World War II from its once-neutral position. All production of civil aircraft had to be stopped immediately in favor of military equipment.

It was the livery of neither TWA nor PAA but the olive green of the US Army Air Force (USAAF) that adorned the Constellation prototype with construction number 1961 when it took off on its maiden flight from the Lockheed Air Terminal in Burbank, California, on January 9, 1943. The prototype bore the registration NX25600. Boeing chief test pilot Edmund T. Allen was in command. Because of his experience with large aircraft, Lockheed had borrowed him from its competitor in Seattle specifically for the Constellation flight tests. Lockheed chief test pilot Milo Burcham assisted Allen in the copilot's seat. Other crew members included flight engineer R. L. Thoren and mechanic Dick Stanton. Lockheed chief developer Kelly Johnson also sat in the well-filled Connie cockpit as an observer. True to the motto "If it looks right, it flies right," the C-69 was so easy to handle right from the start that the test team took off on six test flights on the first day, with a total flight time of two hours and nine minutes. More test flights followed until all aircraft were temporarily grounded on February 20, 1943. Test pilot Eddy Allen had had a fatal accident with the prototype Boeing B-29 Superfortress, the cause of which was quickly traced to a fatal design flaw in its Wright R-3350 engines. This indirectly affected the C-69, which also had to be grounded. Lockheed bridged the wait for improved engines with extensive modifications to the

Lineup of C-69s at the Lockheed factory in Burbank prior to their delivery to the US Army Air Force. *Lockheed Martin*

The military C-69 differed in only a few respects from the civilian L-049 commercial airliner later derived from it. *Lockheed Martin*

Shown here is the L-049 with the registration NC86500, which was delivered to TWA in November 1945. *Lockheed Martin*

aircraft until the arrival of new R-3350 engines made it possible to resume flight testing in June 1943.

This L-049/C-69 was officially handed over to the USAAF on July 28, 1943, during its sixty-fourth test flight, as the first of 260 troop transports ordered—but was immediately returned to Lockheed for further flight tests. Although Howard Hughes had ceded all forty of Transcontinental & Western Air's delivery positions for the Model 49 to the USAAF, he would not have been the enfant terrible of aviation if he had not succeeded in a special PR coup with the second C-69 produced. On its delivery flight to the USAAF from Burbank to Washington, DC, instead of military camouflage colors, the Constellation flew in full TWA livery. With Howard Hughes in command and TWA president Jack Frye as copilot, plus four other crew members and twelve passengers aboard, the plane took off from Burbank at 3:56 a.m. local time on April 17, 1944, and reached the US capital nonstop in a record time of six hours and fifty-eight minutes. This beat Hughes's own transcontinental speed record, set seven years earlier, by 5.31 mph; he had flown between Burbank and Newark in seven hours and twenty-eight minutes in the Hughes H-1 racing plane. His average airspeed was 331.5 miles (533.06 km) per hour. What only a highly bred racing aircraft was capable of on January 19, 1937, could now be undercut by a standard production air transport. There could be no more convincing proof of the progress in aircraft design and the performance of the Connie and its engines.

By the spring of 1945, the USAAF order had grown to seventy-three C-69s, twenty-three of which left final assembly by the time of the armistice. At the end of the war, the US military immediately canceled its acceptance of the remaining fifty aircraft. Lockheed was now faced with the choice of developing a new civilian version of the C-69, which would not be available for a few years, or converting the C-69s from the canceled military order, which were in various stages of construction and planning, into civilian aircraft. Bob Gross opted for the latter alternative. These converted C-69s received their American civil certification as Lockheed L-049s on December 11, 1945.

In late 1945, deliveries of these converted military transports began to the two launch customers from prewar days: TWA and PAA. Other aircraft went to American Overseas Airlines, Air France, BOAC, and KLM. On April 16, 1946, an L-049 Constellation of the PAA subsidiary Panair do Brasil was the first aircraft of a foreign airline to touch down on the runway of London Airport, which had been opened only a few days earlier. The airport was later renamed Heathrow and has been a byword for intercontinental air traffic for decades. Once again, it was an L-049 with which BOAC first took off from London on May 28, 1946, on the kangaroo service offered jointly with QANTAS, bound for Australia. Travel time: almost sixty hours! Pan American Airways finally did the honors for the first time on June 1 with the arrival of its L-049 Clipper London from New York in the Constellation's premiere year of 1946.

From the L-049, via the L-649 and L-749, development finally led to the L-749A, the model with the highest performance of the original Constellation series. It had even-more-powerful engines, a longer range, and higher takeoff weights than its predecessors. More-advanced engines eventually enabled the construction of the L-1049 Super Constellation and L-1649A Starliner.

The original 1939 Clarence "Kelly" Johnson design had so much development potential that it could be stretched and fitted with new wings and turboprop engines. A total of 856 examples of what is probably the most beautiful icon of aircraft design left the final assembly line in Burbank, California, between 1943 and 1958.

This in-flight photo of the Constellation reveals its perfect aerodynamic layout. *Lockheed Martin*

Final assembly of the C-69 in Burbank. *Lockheed Martin*

Dramatic view of a C-69 from an unusual perspective. *Lockheed Martin*

CHAPTER 2 THE CONNIE COMES OF AGE

THE DEVELOPMENTAL HISTORY OF A UNIQUE DESIGN

LOCKHEED CONSTELLATION

With the more powerful and luxuriously appointed L-649 and L-749 versions, Lockheed established the Constellation's reputation as the queen of the skies. But the road was rocky, because after initial euphoria, Lockheed's management feared the high development and production costs associated with the further development of the basic model. Yet, after Japan's surrender in September 1945, the way seemed paved for delivering the prewar orders from TWA and PAA as a so-called "Postwar 049" version. Lockheed board member and chief engineer Hall Hibbard went a step further when he pitched what he called the "Gold Plated L-049" variant to TWA management as the "most luxurious aircraft with the longest range and best performance in the sky." Hibbard proposed as its power plant four Wright 3350 engines, which had sufficient power reserves for future, larger Constellation versions. The cabin, on the other hand, was to be produced with improved air-conditioning over the C-69, and an opulent interior including berths that folded out of the ceiling.

In anticipation of the coming of peacetime, TWA and Lockheed signed a supplementary agreement on November 14, 1944, for ten of these postwar 049s, which were to become part of the original contract. The contracting parties did not plan to finalize their exact specifications until 1945, in order to be able to integrate as many as possible of the rapid technical advances then taking place into the design of the new machines. In addition, TWA hoped to be able to use technologies that were still under military secrecy during the war for the new Constellation in the dawning peacetime.

GREAT DISENCHANTMENT

Lockheed found itself in a dilemma, because with the production of civil aircraft starting up again in the summer of 1945, the exclusive contract signed with Howard Hughes in 1939 acted as a brake. Airlines around the globe showed great interest in the "postwar 049," but Lockheed was not allowed to negotiate seriously with any of them. Lockheed

The C-69s of the US Army Air Force were primarily operated as troop transports during the Second World War. *Lockheed Martin*

CEO Bob Gross initially tried in vain to persuade Hughes to relax this clause in the contract—and TWA finally gave in to Lockheed's urging and agreed to allow it to sell to other customers. In addition to its interest in the "gold-plated" L-049, TWA was willing to accept "commercial C-69s" converted to passenger aircraft at minimal cost as a temporary solution. These aircraft were no longer needed by the US Air Force as transport aircraft immediately after Japan's surrender and were thus available to the airline on short notice. For the more luxurious postwar 049, on the other hand, Lockheed built a cabin mockup in Burbank in which the equipment details that TWA wanted on the improved Connie were presented to airline management for production approval. Everything was ready for the final contract signing when Hall Hibbard summoned the TWA managers involved in aircraft selection to Burbank in August 1945 to announce the end of the postwar 049 project. The dismayed TWA employees had to be told that it was easier and less expensive for Lockheed to keep the C-69 production line running with minimal effort than to add the production of an improved version of the Constellation. Moreover, except for the passenger seats, the newly built L-049s were to offer no more cabin comfort than the military C-69s. Now TWA was in a quandary because the airline was bound, for better or worse, to Lockheed on the basis of its purchase contract for forty aircraft. The option of purchasing the Douglas DC-6, which was superior technically, economically, and in terms of passenger comfort, was therefore ruled out from the outset. Even a list of requested technical changes compared to the military C-69, which TWA classified as safety relevant, was only partially accepted by Lockheed. Other items, such as optimized nosewheel steering and air-conditioning, had to be developed and installed by the TWA engineering department itself in its workshops.

By November 1945, Lockheed had booked orders for eighty-nine L-049s from TWA, PAA, American Overseas Airlines, the Brazilian PAA subsidiary Panair do Brasil, the Dutch airline KLM, and Air France. Nevertheless, competitive pressure from the technologically and economically far-superior Douglas DC-6 became so great that Lockheed finally cleared the way for an improved Constellation, designated the Model 649, in January 1946. To the delight of Howard Hughes, the modification package for the first true postwar Constellation developed exclusively for the civil aviation market included almost all the items TWA had already negotiated with Lockheed the summer before. Among them were the luxurious cabin interior, improved air-conditioning and pressurized cabin system, modernized cockpit, a higher maximum takeoff weight, and more-powerful Wright R-3350 Duplex Cyclone engines with a maximum of 2,500—instead of 2,200—horsepower for takeoff. The L-649 was so promising that TWA converted a September 14, 1945, order for eighteen L-049s into an equal number of L-649s within a few weeks. The prototype "Gold Plated L-049" took off from Burbank on its maiden flight on October 19, 1946. Besides TWA, Eastern Air Lines was the only customer for this interim version, after Lockheed had already announced the further-improved L-749 in the spring of 1947. Thus, all other potential buyers opted for that upgraded version. Eastern Air Lines put the first L-649 into service on the New York–Miami route in June 1947.

TWA took delivery of its first brand-new Model 049 at Burbank on November 14, 1945. After a promotional flight on December 3 of that year, Transcontinental & Western Air opened regular service between New York and Paris on February 5, 1946. The L-049, appropriately christened "Star of Paris," took off from New York's La Guardia Airport bound for Paris-Orly under the command of Captain Hall Blackburn. The next international destinations for TWA's L-049s soon followed—Rome on April 2 and, shortly thereafter, Cairo. Howard Hughes personally commanded the Star of California on its inaugural flight from Los Angeles to New York on February 15, 1946. On board were thirty-five Hollywood stars from the circle of acquaintances of the TWA owner, who also enjoyed legendary fame as a film producer. Among them were Cary Grant, William Powell, and Tyrone Power.

Buy War Bonds

THE TWA SKYLINER

Buy War Bonds

Vol. 6, No. 3 — Published by TRANSCONTINENTAL & WESTERN AIR, INC. — MARCH, 1942

War Role Goes to Stratoliners in New Setup

Otis Bryan Commands Crew on First Flight

When incoming flight 20 wheeled up to the ramp at LG Field the evening of March 14, it rang down the curtain for the duration on scheduled Stratoliner flights. Transfer of the entire four-engine fleet to the U. S. Army was near completion.

In the meantime the first Stratoliner had taken off with its TWA crew for foreign fronts. The former luxury ship, garbed in full war paint, bore the proud insignia of the Air Corps Ferrying Command, for whom the newly created Intercontinental Division of TWA is operating under contract. A key to the importance of the operation is contained in the ACFC insignia, which means "From West to East with greatest possible speed."

On hand to bid the crew Godspeed were Civil Aeronautics Board members, TWA officials and other dignitaries. Crew members on the epochal opening flight of the foreign courier service were Capt. Otis Bryan, who was in command of the plane; Milo Campbell and Donald Terry, first officers; Peter H. Redpath and Guy Arnold, navigators; W. L. Noftsinger, second officer; W. R. Shook, radio operator and Robert L. Proctor, flight engineer.

The Stratoliners, the nation's greatest transport planes, went into scheduled service over the TWA system July 8, 1940, eleven years to the day from the inaugural coast-to-coast "air and rail" service of old Transcontinental Air Transport, predecessor of TWA.

On their initial flights the revolutionary Boeings posted new transcontinental transport speed records of 12 hours and 13 minutes eastbound and 14 hours and 9 minutes westbound, ushering in a new era of luxury air transportation.

TWA, in a brief six-year span, has introduced two transports to the world that have greatly influenced aviation history. Another, the Constellation, is being readied!

The Douglas, presented to an eager public in 1934, brought increased dependability, speed, comfort and safety to air travel. The Stratoliner, with the added safety factor of four engines and upper level flight, carried the refinements on to greater heights. And the forthcoming Lockheed Constellation will surpass all transport aircraft heretofore flown.

Credited to the Stratoliners are far-reaching developments in the progress of commercial transport aviation.

They were the first "over-weather" supercharged cabin planes to go into passenger service anywhere in the world; they were the first 4-engine planes to be successfully operated on domestic airline schedules; they completed a new air highway between the Orient and Europe, enabling passengers to travel by air in giant four-engine airliners from Europe to the Far East via Pan American and TWA in six days actual flying time; they shortened materially the distance between the Atlantic and Pacific Coast and between many key cities.

The inauguration of Stratoliner service over TWA's route, where the old TAT line blazed the first transcontinental air trail ten years before, climaxed a decade of growth in air transportation in which TWA pioneered dozens of major developments.

Before TWA accepted the Stratoliner, it was put through the most rigid test ever given any commercial air transport, and engineers pronounced it the most perfect transport plane built up to that time. Prior to this TWA had completed years of exhaustive experimental researches into high altitude operation under the direction of President Jack Frye, Executive Vice President Paul Richter, and D. W. Tomlinson, now on leave with the Navy. The famous Northrop Gamma "Flying Laboratory" was used for this purpose.

The files in the passenger relations department are crammed with hundreds of letters from passengers attesting to the comfort of Stratoliner travel.

Invaluable experience was gained in cabin supercharging and four-engine operation. This knowledge has benefited TWA, the industry, and the armed forces too, as witnessed by the Jack Frye four-engine school at Albuquerque. The Stratoliners established an enviable record. In just a little over one year and seven months, the five-plane fleet rolled up a total of more than 4,600,000 miles—a high tribute to their construction and rating TWA's operating and maintenance methods.

Members of the Civil Aeronautics Board were present at the inaugural take-off of the first Stratoliner—with crew—recently turned over to the Army to serve in a foreign courier service. Pictured above (L to R) are: Standing—N. S. Talbott, TWA director; Oswald Ryan, C. A. B.; Peter Redpath, navigator; Donald Terry, first officer; President Jack Frye; Otis Bryan, captain; Milo Campbell, first officer; W. L. Noftsinger, second officer; George Baker, C. A. B.; kneeling—Harllee Branch, C. A. B.; Wesley Pogue, chairman, C. A. B.; W. R. Shook, radio operator; Robert L. Proctor, flight engineer; Guy Arnold, navigator; Edward P. Warner, C. A. B.

THE NATION'S NEWEST AND MIGHTIEST AIR TRANSPORT

The Lockheed Constellation, designed and built for TWA, will be test flown at the Lockheed plant at Burbank, Calif., this summer, it has been announced by Jack Frye (right inset), who with Howard Hughes (left inset) conceived the ultra-modern transport. Here are the first pictures of the airliner, built to fly from LA to NY in 8½ hours at altitudes above 25,000 feet and at cruising speeds of nearly 300 miles an hour. The plane carries 57 passengers and a crew of seven. The above is a wind-tunnel model.

Richter Rates Safety First in All Operations

Van Skike's and Kay's Departments Honored

The engine overhaul and radio and electrical departments won top honors in the 1941 TWA Accident Prevention contest, according to figures just released by the Health and Safety Department.

In presenting a plaque to G. F. Van Skike, foreman of engine overhaul and a certificate to Keith Kay, radio and electrical foreman, Executive Vice-President Richter stressed the importance at this time of an alert program of accident prevention.

All maintenance personnel stopped work for 15 minutes the afternoon of March 11 to witness the presentation of the awards. On hand to represent the company in addition to Mr. Richter, were Personnel Manager L. M. Reed and R. G. Bloomer, supervisor of the health and safety department.

"Stopping work in a group like this and bringing them together for a few minutes means a considerable time loss," Mr. Richter pointed out, "but we have done so to emphasize our interest in industrial accident prevention.

"Posters, circulars, and bulletins have told you how important to TWA, to the aviation industry, and to our country is the conservation of man power, materials, and equipment through the elimination of waste from accidents.

"Nobody is being asked to do anything in this campaign of conservation that causes any extra effort on his part, or is not for his own personal good. When a man is injured in an accident everybody loses, but the man that gets hurt loses most of all."

Mr. Richter noted that a substantial reduction of industrial accidents was made in the maintenance department during the past year and declared that the company was proud that TWA had been awarded a plaque for winning the 1941 Accident Prevention Contest among Kansas City industries of similar risks.

"Nobody can contribute much to win this war from a hospital bed or a wheel chair," he warned. "Through everybody doing his individual job in a safe and efficient manner, we will be helping a lot toward getting this war won."

Ranking in order behind engine overhaul and radio and electrical in the safety contest were the following departments: instruments, miscellaneous overhaul, plane and engine service, cleaners, propellor.

Mr. Bloomer, in answer to a question as to the formula used in rating the various maintenance departments, said that the records of

(Continued on page 8, col. 1)

Left: In its March 1942 issue, the TWA staff newspaper, the TWA Skyliner, announced the first flight of the Constellation, which it was hoped would take place in the summer, with a photo of a model that did not yet depict the final version. In fact, the C-69 prototype did not take off on its maiden flight until January 9, 1943. And TWA did not receive its first aircraft until 1945. *Author's collection*

From left to right: propliners, manufactured by Lockheed, Douglas and Convair dominated the skies of the Western world in the 1940s and 1950s. *ETH Zurich*

TWA's former L-049 "Star of Switzerland" was built in 1945 as a C-69 for the US Air Force. Today, it is on display at the Pima Air and Space Museum, Arizona, after extensive restoration. *John Bezosky, collections and restoration manager, Pima Air and Space Museum*

SOLO EFFORT

All the glamor could not hide the fact that TWA was in financial trouble—which culminated in the cancellation of the long-awaited but unaffordable L-649 in March 1947. For TWA, this was a disaster. First Lockheed refused to produce the improved L-049, only to offer the L-649 after all, which TWA ultimately could not pay for. It was not until 1948 that the airline's coffers were so well filled again that it put twelve of the aircraft it had originally ordered, parked in the meantime by Lockheed at Burbank, into service as further-improved L-749s. In order to have not only an equivalent but a better aircraft than the Douglas DC-6, TWA management also showed interest in the L-749A version. Lockheed offered this new long-range aircraft with a 2.3-ton increase in takeoff weight, greater fuel capacity and range, improved wheel brakes, and piston engines less prone to icing—and these were only the most-significant improvements. Douglas's response in the form of the DC-6B was not long in coming, and fierce competition between the two California aircraft manufacturers for the prestigious TWA contract ensued. The die already seemed to have been cast in favor of the DC-6B as Trans World Airlines' new long-range aircraft, which according to internal calculations by TWA specialists was superior to the L-749A in all commercial and technical respects. Nevertheless, Howard Hughes, in one of his legendary solo efforts not even agreed upon with his closest associates, placed an order on May 31, 1949, for an initial twenty L-749As for delivery the following year, which was shortly thereafter augmented by five more L-749As for delivery in 1951. Three more aircraft, originally produced for Delta Air Lines but not accepted, completed the TWA L-749A fleet. Nevertheless, in retrospect, Trans World Airlines had no reason to regret its major shareholder's initially inexplicable decision in favor of the Lockheed product and successfully operated its L-749As for a period of seventeen years until they were replaced by the first jets.

A POLE IS IN THE WAY

The capriciousness of Howard Hughes sometimes demanded strong nerves not only from his closest confidants but also from his business partners. This was revealed by the example of his private L-749A. The aircraft was in the Lockheed final-assembly hangar in 1951 and was ready for its first flight tests when Hughes had it locked up by armed guards on the Lockheed company premises, which he was not in the least entitled to do. Even the pleas from Lockheed chief Bob Gross, whose Constellation production line was stalled, could not persuade the eccentric aviator to change his mind. We can only speculate about the background to this unusual behavior, which Hughes repeated years later at Convair on the CV-880 final-assembly line. One night Hughes appeared without notice at the Lockheed factory airfield along with a flight engineer, started the engines of the L-749A with the registration N6025C, and taxied across the Lockheed Aircraft Corporation apron in the dark without permission. He missed by a hair's breadth a pole standing in the way, which brought the taxi maneuver, which had been arranged with no one, to an abrupt halt. Again, Hughes had his aircraft, now sitting in the middle of the apron, locked down by armed guards and forbade that it be towed backward to a safe location. Finally, Lockheed gave in to the muscle flexing and dug the pole out of the ground, and Hughes allowed the Constellation to be towed nose first to a protective hangar. There it remained for three years, until Hughes sold his private, never-flown L-749A in August 1954 to the British airline BOAC, which registered its aircraft G-ANNT and christened it "Buckingham."

LOCKHEED SUPER CONSTELLATION

Following the L-749A, the next generation of the Constellation series was launched on October 13, 1950, in the form of the Lockheed L-1049 Super Constellation. It would become the bestseller of all the versions of the Connie. It was

The Constellation on display at the Dutch Aviodrome Museum at Lelystad is in the historic colors of KLM. *Wolfgang Borgmann*

A passenger cabin with pure first-class seating arrangement of an L-649. *Lockheed Martin*

An L-749 of Air India International taking off from Zurich's then international airport at Dübendorf. *ETH Zurich*

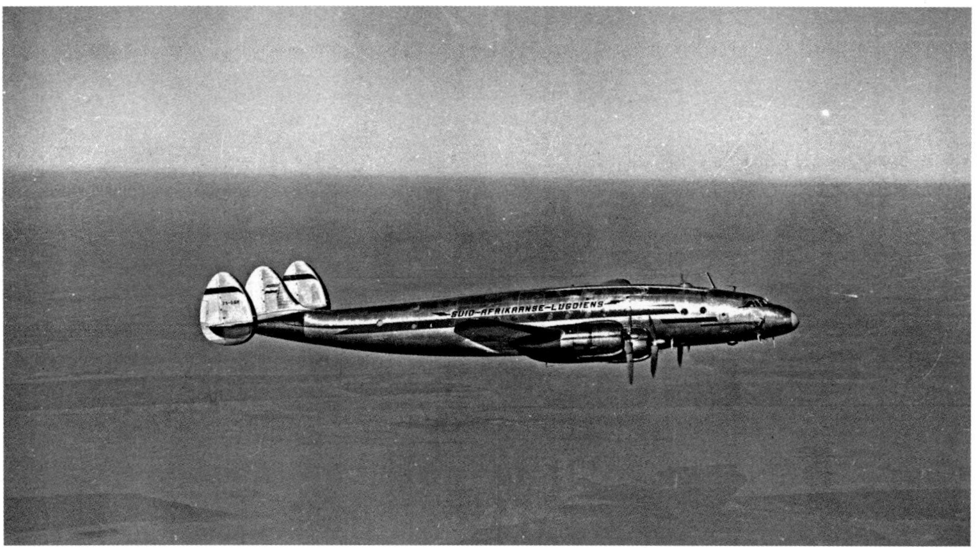

The South African Airways L-749A with the registration ZS-DBR shown here was the South African airline's first Constellation and was flown by the airline from August 1950 to November 1958. *THL Image Collection / SAR Publicity and Travel Department*

Promotional photo taken in 1944 by Lockheed for Transcontinental & Western Air Inc., depicting a Lockheed C-69 and a Lockheed Model 18 Lodestar. *Lockheed Martin*

Burbank's answer to the DC-6B of Lockheed's Californian archrival Douglas. Lockheed had invited TWA, as an early customer, to become actively involved in the development of the L-1049. Both parties would have benefited—Lockheed from the day-to-day experience of an airline, while TWA would have been given a unique opportunity to obtain a long-range aircraft tailored to its requirements. TWA, however, had done the math without its wayward major shareholder, Howard Hughes. When it was time to contract with Lockheed for the detailed solutions TWA wanted, Hughes disappeared without a trace for several months and did not respond to attempts by his airline managers to contact him by letter or telephone. So, it was Eastern Air Lines that ordered the first ten aircraft for its low-cost domestic routes on the US East Coast on April 24, 1950. Eastern took delivery of the first of the fourteen Super Constellations it had ordered on November 26, 1951. It was not until four months after the Eastern order that Howard Hughes returned to his team and asked them to negotiate a purchase contract with Lockheed for ten aircraft for TWA virtually overnight. With the aircraft design now finalized and Lockheed unwilling to accept TWA's special requests for cockpit instrumentation and cabin interiors, the Kansas City–based airline was forced to order L-1049s built to Eastern Air Lines standards. For example, Lockheed resorted to the less powerful air-conditioning system of the smaller L-749A, designed for thirty fewer passengers, for the L-1049 due to cost considerations. The only difference between the Eastern L-1049s used on short shuttle flights and those TWA's Super Constellations intended for long routes of nearly ten flying hours was the color of the passenger seats and those of the carpets and side panels in the cabin. Thus, after this debacle, there was not only "tension in the air" on board, but also between the TWA fleet buyers and Howard Hughes.

The aircraft chosen as the prototype of the L-1049 was an old acquaintance, because Lockheed made it easy for itself and stretched the fuselage of the C-69 prototype built in 1943 with the construction number 1961 by 3.3 feet to produce the first Super Connie. Before that, however, the manufacturer had to buy back the original prototype, sold to Howard Hughes in 1946 for $25,000, for $100,000. To save time, the Pratt & Whitney R-2800 engines that had been installed in the meantime remained on the aircraft at the start of flight testing. Only after twenty-two hours of flight did the Lockheed test team replace the 1961 engines with the more powerful R-3350 Wright Cyclone C18 CA1 production engines. At 2,700 hp, the output of these twin-row radial engines was still far below that of the R-3350 turbocompound versions of later L-1049 and L-1649A variants, which produced a maximum of 3,400 hp. Their three power recovery turbines (PRTs) per engine were coupled to the engine's crankshaft via various reduction gears for the purpose of power recovery and were driven by the hot and very fast stream of exhaust gases and thus contributed directly to the power increase of the unit.

Since the US military initially claimed the new turbocompound technology for itself, it was not available for the civilian Super Constellation until 1953. Thus, the 3,250 hp Wright Cyclone R-3350-972-TC18DA-1 turbocompound engines were first used on an L-1049C operated by the Dutch airline KLM. At the time of its maiden flight on February 17, 1953, Lockheed had already received orders for seventy Constellations of this variant. It was followed by the L-1049D combi version, which was unpopular with airlines and of which only four entered service with Seaboard & Western Airlines (S&W) from 1954. Converted to passenger aircraft, two L-1049Ds leased by S&W flew for a time on the route network of the British airline BOAC from London to Bermuda and New York.

By far the most successful model in the Super Constellation series, however, was the L-1049G. Its development was once again forced by fierce competition with Douglas, whose DC-7 flew faster than the best Super Constellation model up to that time. Since speed was a key selling point for airlines at the time, Douglas DC-7 customers American Airlines and United Air Lines in particular boasted of this competitive advantage over their rivals' L-1049 fleets—most notably Trans World Airlines. Thus, on November 29, 1953, American inaugurated its DC-7 Mercury service between New York and Los Angeles

Lockheed bought the prototype of the Lockheed Constellation back from Howard Hughes and lengthened its fuselage to produce the Super Constellation prototype. *Lockheed Martin*

The TWA L-1049 "Star of the Seine" shown in this Lockheed factory photo taken in 1952 collided with a United Air Lines DC-7 at this exact spot on June 30, 1956. All 128 people on both aircraft lost their lives. *Lockheed Martin*

in direct competition with TWA's slower L-1049 Ambassador service. Even the Lockheed Model 1049E, ordered by TWA in 1953 in response to the DC-7, could not match the cruise speed of its fast Douglas competitor. Lockheed was well aware of this precarious situation and finally developed the L-1049G, a version equal to the DC-7 for the first time, with further increased fuel capacity, range, and speed. TWA converted its order for twenty L-1049Es into the improved G model, thus becoming the launch customer for this successful variant. With its distinctive wingtip fuel tanks, which Lockheed had adopted from the US Navy's R7V-1 military variant, its elegant appearance contributed much to the Lockheed Super Constellation myth. The Super G, on the other hand, owed its dubious reputation as the "most reliable three-engined aircraft ever built" to the susceptibility of its four Curtiss-Wright R-3350 engines to failure. All too often, the graceful aircraft reached their destinations after a transatlantic flight with only three working engines—and one shut down.

The L-1049G was certified for flight on January 14, 1955, and the 104 examples of this bestselling Super Constellation type that were built were among the flagships of the fleet for many years, not only at TWA.

In June 1955, Lockheed announced the development of another variant, called the L-1049H. This combination version could be used both as a freighter and in passenger service. Flying Tiger Line was the first customer for this last civilian version of the L-1049, which was equipped with R-3350-972-TC18EA-3 turbocompound engines, each producing 3,400 hp for takeoff. This meant that this piston engine technology of the propeller age had reached its peak. From the end of the 1950s, more-reliable jet engines enabled the Super Connies to be removed from the main routes of world air traffic, and their zenith thus lasted only a few years.

LOCKHEED STARLINER

Just one year before the start of the long-haul jet age, Lockheed launched the L-1649A Starliner, the most powerful of all Constellation versions, in 1957. Thus, the L-1649A heralded the grand finale of piston engine commercial aircraft operating between Europe and North America. Earlier versions of the Constellation series were already regarded as pioneers of global air transport, but it was to the forty-four L-1649As produced that the honor of literally opening new horizons was due. The Starliner was the first commercial aircraft capable of flying the distance between the Old and New Worlds nonstop, without the refueling stops required by older models. This reduced flight times for the traveling public by several hours! But even this remarkable advance paled into insignificance with the advent of the jet age over the North Atlantic in 1958. Within a few years, jet aircraft, which were almost twice as fast, were vibration-free, and flew above the weather, ousted the magnificent transatlantic propeller-driven airliners from the main routes and ended this fascinating era of air travel for all time.

The Lockheed L-1649A was an unloved child from the start. Fleet planners at TWA, the launch customer, rejected it as uneconomical because Boeing and Douglas were already working on prototypes of their four-engine 707 and DC-8 jets. Even Lockheed tried to prevent production at the last second by canceling the sales contract with TWA because it saw no sales opportunities. Only aviation tycoon Howard Hughes, at that time owner of TWA, persistently held on to his order for the final version of the legendary Constellation series, against the advice of his closest confidants.

Development of the L-1649A with Curtiss-Wright piston engines initially began as a turboprop with the type designation L-1449. It was intended to make TWA competitive again with the Douglas DC-7Cs operated by other airlines. Announced in 1954, the Douglas Seven Seas surpassed TWA's Lockheed L-1049G, and not just in terms of cruising speed. Its long range also eliminated the need for refueling stops on the route between the United States and Europe and on routes between the East and West Coasts of the United States.

Fearing competitive disadvantages, TWA management initially considered ordering DC-7Cs themselves when rumors began to circulate that Lockheed was working on a

A Lufthansa L-1049G on final approach to the Hamburg-Fuhlsbüttel airport, whose name is painted on the roof of a hangar. *Hamburg Airport*

This great shot of a TWA Jetstream really shows the dimensions of the L-1649A. *Neil Higgins*

The Starliner prototype, which first flew on October 10, 1956, during the L-1649A flight test program. *Lockheed Martin*

For many Constellation fans the L-1649A represents the most elegant version of the original design. *Lockheed Martin*

"long thin wing" for a turboprop version of the Constellation. It would provide not only higher cruise speeds but also a range comparable to that of the DC-7C—and the L-1449 project was born. In the fall of 1954, Howard Hughes decided to purchase twenty-five of these aircraft, projected with four Pratt & Whitney T-34 turboprops, for TWA through his Hughes Tool Company. This was spelled out in a purchase agreement signed on Christmas Eve 1954. After a close look at the operating costs calculated by Lockheed for the turboprop ordered by Hughes, TWA managers were shocked. In their opinion, TWA would not make a single dollar of profit on the L-1449. But the arguments they presented to Howard Hughes were of no avail. He wanted to buy the L-1449 no matter what—and even against the advice and better arguments from his TWA team.

The ink on the purchase contract had not quite dried when Lockheed chief designer Kelly Johnson reported to TWA on January 7, 1955, with bad news: flight tests of the R7V-2 test aircraft had shown that the engine-propeller combination of the T-34 engine did not work. And even worse: there was no economically viable solution to the problems. Just a few weeks after this initial alarming news, Pratt & Whitney officially ended development of the T-34 turboprop—and the L-1449 project suddenly found itself without propulsion. Lockheed tried to save what could no longer be saved with the L-1549 model, but none of the turboprop alternatives available at the time were considered a truly suitable replacement. The engines were either too large, available too late, or not yet ready for production. Parallel studies by TWA and Lockheed showed that the only way forward could be a replacement of the turboprops with conventional Curtiss-Wright 3350 EA-2 turbocompound piston engines, in combination with large-diameter, slow-turning propellers. Lockheed now named this model L-1649A and prepared an amendment to the purchase agreement signed with TWA in December 1954 to that effect.

This photo clearly shows how far the stretched wings of the L-1649A bent upward while in cruising flight. *Lufthansa*

Evening atmosphere with a Super Star at the Lufthansa base in Hamburg. *Lufthansa*

Air France, with TWA and Lufthansa the only customers for the L-1649A, called its aircraft the Super Starliner. *Lockheed Martin*

An impressive size comparison between the L-1649A (*below*) and Super Constellation. *Lockheed Martin*

LOCKHEED PLANS TO GET OUT

Into this tense situation burst the news from Howard Hughes, which he once again had not discussed with TWA management, that he was demanding a retrofit of the TWA L-1049G fleet with additional Westinghouse J-34 jet engines to increase their cruising speed. Only with difficulty could he be dissuaded by hastily prepared analyses by TWA and Lockheed, which in unison showed no economic benefit. With the Super Constellation jet retrofit off the table again, TWA converted its order for twenty-five L-1449s to the identical number of L-1649As by a contract amendment dated March 29, 1955. The Starliner was thus officially launched, but the change in the construction plans now required also moved the delivery time of the aircraft destined for TWA into 1957 and 1958—and thus ever closer to the imminent jet age on long-haul routes. Thus, TWA management was surprised, but on the other hand also pleased, when Lockheed, in a letter dated April 6, 1955,

Rollout of the first L-1649A from the final-assembly line at Burbank. *Lockheed Martin*

Formation flight of a TWA Jetstream and a navy WV-2. *Lockheed Martin*

officially declared the L-1649A project terminated. Lockheed had obviously concluded that the Starliner had no chance against the faster jets. TWA management, too, now freed from the burden of the unwelcome propeller-driven aircraft, hoped to launch into a jet-only future with the preferred Boeing 707. But both parties had done the math without taking Howard Hughes into account. The erratic TWA owner insisted on contract performance, to the frustration of his own team and the manufacturer—and Lockheed was forced to put the L-1649A into production. In the spring of 1955, TWA placed an order for twenty-five L-1649A-98s, the number 98 representing the engine variant, officially signaling the start of Starliner development. The Lockheed managers' worst fears were soon to be realized. In addition to the twenty-five aircraft Lockheed built for TWA, only two other customers for new L-1649As were found: Air France and Lufthansa.

Flight trials began on October 10, 1956, with the prototype's maiden flight from the Lockheed Air Terminal in Burbank. The Starliner received its type certificate on March 19, 1957, and just six weeks later Lockheed delivered the first aircraft to TWA, which sent it on its maiden flight on the New York–Paris route on June 1, 1957. It was also TWA that operated the longest scheduled flight without a refueling stop with a Starliner. On this route from the British capital London to San Francisco, California, a TWA L-1649A set a new record of twenty-three hours and nineteen minutes on October 1, 1957.

The fact that these extreme long-haul flights stretched not only people but also equipment to their limits is demonstrated by TWA's use of a Fairchild C-82A Packet, which it employed exclusively to transport engines from 1957 onward. Its sole task was to transport defective Connie engines for repair, and spare engines for broken-down L-1649As and L-1049Gs on TWA's route network around the globe. The Packet was in continuous service even after the service entry of the first versions of the Boeing 707 jetliner, whose engines were also not very reliable, until 1972!

In addition to the original order for twenty-five L-1649As, TWA also took over four delivery positions from Italy's Linee Aeree Italiane, which it had returned to Lockheed after the merger with Douglas customer Alitalia. After Brazil's Varig converted a letter of intent to purchase two L-1649As into firm orders for three L-1049Gs, only Air France—with ten—and Lufthansa—with four—placed further orders for the Starliner. In all, just forty-four examples left the final-assembly line in Burbank, California. None of the three customers for new L-1649As operated their aircraft under the Starliner name specified by Lockheed. Air France, for example, called its aircraft the Super Starliner, Lufthansa called its new flagship the Super Star, and Trans World Airlines marketed its aircraft as the Jetstream, or Radar Jetstream if they were equipped with the then-novel in-flight weather radar.

"MISTER STARLINER," MAURICE ROUNDY

The story of the Lockheed L-1649A would not be complete without another name: Maurice Roundy. Like no other, he linked his destiny to three L-1649As he purchased. A commercial pilot, flight instructor, flight engineer, mechanic, and aviation examiner, Roundy found his "Connie calling" some five decades ago. His enthusiasm was triggered by an article in an American aviation magazine about the Constellation series. Roundy quickly chose the L-1649A as his particular favorite among the members of the Connie, Super Connie, and Starliner family.

As a commercial pilot at the time, he flew charter companies' jets all over the United States. This gave him the chance to look for the last surviving Lockheed propeller-driven airliners even in remote places. After many years of dreaming of his own Starliner, Maurice Roundy finally found himself financially able to fulfill his long-cherished wish in the early 1980s. On the basis of his years of research, he knew exactly where to find the last three airworthy examples in the United States and Honduras.

A Lufthansa L-1649A in the foreground and, behind it, one of the airline's L-1049Gs. *Lufthansa*

View of the New York City skyline from the cabin window of a Lufthansa L-1649A. *Lufthansa*

Cutaway drawing of the L-1649A's cabin from the year 1957. *Lufthansa*

Maurice Roundy in front of one of his L-1649As. It was flown by Lufthansa as D-ALAN and is now on display at the Fantasy of Flight Museum in Florida. *Maurice Roundy*

In June 1983, Maurice Roundy first acquired the aircraft with the construction number 1018 and the registration N7316C. It was officially owned by Maine Coast Airways, which had been established in 1973 as a so-called FBO (fixed base operator), who offered ground-handling operations for the business aviation. This former TWA Jetstream was followed in 1985 by the former D-ALAN of Lufthansa with the construction number 1040, and last but not least in 1986 by the former TWA aircraft construction number 1038 with the registration N8083H. At times, Maurice Roundy's three children were involved with the aircraft. In a display of gratitude, the L-1649As were christened Jenny's Star (N974R), Brian's Star (N8083H), and Jason's Star (N7316C).

For many years, Maurice Roundy's friend and fellow professional pilot Philip J. Kemp provided advice and support in planning the commercial use of the three Starliners. But even together, despite many good ideas, they were unable to find a sponsor for the airworthy restoration of one L-1649A—or all three.

Nevertheless, Maurice Roundy refused to give up and at least preserved the technical status quo of the three Starliners, thus saving them from otherwise certain decay. This always in the hope that one day his dream of a flying an L-1649A would come true.

After a quarter of a century of futile searching for a sponsor, the maintenance of the three Lockheed propeller-driven airliners, which not only cost money but brought in nothing, had driven Maurice Roundy into financial ruin.

Early in 2007, the author of this book took the initiative in this seemingly hopeless situation. Together with retired Lufthansa flight captain and former Starliner pilot Didi Krauss, the idea was born to bring one of the aircraft back to Germany as a Lufthansa "tradition aircraft." After a year of secretive preparation, the intensive efforts in the second half of 2007 finally led to the longed-for breakthrough—or so thought all the protagonists involved in this deal at the time. By purchasing the three L-1649As from Maurice Roundy's private bankruptcy estate, his life's work was transferred first to the Deutsche Lufthansa Berlin Foundation, and later to the nonprofit Lufthansa Super Star gGmbH. But unfortunately, even after ten years of effort, the attempt to restore it, including certification as a commercial aircraft with pressurized cabin for long-haul enthusiast flights, had failed.

THE ADVENTUROUS LIFE STORIES OF THE STARLINER

N7316C began its long life in June 1957 as the Trans World Airlines (TWA) Jetstream that the airline christened "Star of the Tigris." After three years of passenger service on TWA's worldwide network, Lockheed Aircraft Service converted the L-1649A into a freighter in the winter of 1960.

Two years as a cargo aircraft in TWA colors were followed by its sale to Alaska Airlines. Thus, from 1962 onward, the L-1649A earned its money over the expanses of the northernmost US state—first as a transporter of all vital goods to the North, and then from 1968 as a flying tanker to supply the state's remote settlements with gasoline.

After a last flight across the Atlantic to Paris, Le Bourget, in 1976, making what was for the time being the last landing by an L-1649A in Europe, the Jetstream was parked at an airfield in New York State. There it was discovered by Maurice Roundy. He bought the L-1649A and on November 9, 1983, flew it to his home airfield in Maine as the first aircraft of the Starliner trio.

The second and, for the time being, the last Starliner of the trio, L-1649A-98-16, with registration N8083H, arrived at Auburn-Lewiston Airport in 1986. It was originally part of an order from Linee Aeree Italiane (LAI) for four Starliners. After their cancellation, TWA took over the delivery positions and operated the four L-1649As beginning in 1958 to supplement the twenty-five L-1649A-98-20 Jetstreams already on firm order. Externally, these ex-LAI aircraft were distinguished in TWA colors by a white-painted radar nose—which, however, did not contain a weather radar. This was in stark contrast to the other TWA Jetstreams, which were equipped with a black nose radome and weather radar. In addition, the four Italians operated by the American airline were not christened with names.

After its use as a passenger aircraft and subsequent conversion to a freighter, TWA sold this propeller-driven airliner to Alaska Airlines in December 1962. Like its sister aircraft N7316C, it was initially used as a freighter, and then as a fuel transport within Alaska. More adventurous, however, was its use for cargo flights in Latin America, where it is rumored to have carried illegal weapons.

In 1984, the Starliner was parked at San Pedro Sula, Honduras, and initially faced an uncertain future. In May 1986, Maurice Roundy's Maine Coast Airways acquired the L-1649A, saving it from certain deterioration. On May 1, 1986, N8083H arrived at Auburn-Lewiston Airport from San Pedro Sula, after a stopover in Fort Lauderdale, Florida.

The subsequent flying career of the former Lufthansa D-ALAN was mostly quiet, except for two attempts to fly the Super Star, now registered N974R, to Auburn, which failed spectacularly in 1988. After Lufthansa's sale of the aircraft to Parker & Ransom Aircraft Sales in 1966, Air Ventures acquired the freighter, now registered N179AV. After it was briefly chartered by Lebanon's Trans Mediterranean Airways (TMA), the Starliner returned to the USA and received its current N974R registration as early as 1967. In July 1976, Lufthansa's former flagship landed at Fort Lauderdale, Florida, without the prospect of a new owner in sight. Had Maurice Roundy not acquired this Starliner in May 1986, the L-1649A-98-17 would probably have been scrapped long ago.

"Adventurous" is perhaps the most apt description for the two futile attempts to ferry the erstwhile D-ALAN in flight to Auburn in 1988. After two and a half years of maintenance by Maurice Roundy and his numerous volunteer helpers, the Starliner appeared to be technically fit for a ferry flight from Fort Lauderdale, Florida, to Auburn, Maine, on August 18, 1988. However, immediately after refueling, the Super Star began leaking in many places. Leaks in the fuel tanks and in the fuel and hydraulic lines had to be stopped before the crew of Captain John McBride, First Officer Philip J. Kemp, flight engineer Ralph Dominguez, and crew chief Ray Porter could safely start the aircraft's four Curtiss-Wright engines. With all available engine power and using the last bit of concrete on the 3,000-foot runway at Fort Lauderdale Airport, the Super Star lifted off to fly north. But they didn't get far, because shortly after takeoff the following scenario presented itself, which copilot Philip J. Kemp described as follows: "We put on an impressive show over the well-attended beaches of West Palm Beach. The jammed nose gear was hanging out, engine number 1 was trailing a cloud of black smoke—all at an altitude of about 2,000 feet [600 m] above the heads of the bathers!" Captain McBride sent a distress call to West Palm Beach Airport, which was dead ahead, and the stricken Super Star landed there safely a short time later. In view of all the aircraft's defects, the tire that blew out during takeoff in Fort Lauderdale, caused by the burst left wheel brake of the main landing gear, hardly mattered. In the five weeks that followed, the team of mechanics, filled with enthusiasm, devoted themselves to the required repair work.

Engine number 1 was repaired at Fort Lauderdale, and the defective tire and brake were replaced. After the problem with the nose gear also seemed to have been solved, the crew decided to make a second attempt to fly to Maine on September 19, 1988. Everything was going suspiciously well, and the crew was convinced that the mission would be a success when, after about an hour of flight, chaos suddenly descended upon the crew. The engines began failing, one after the other, and the number 1 engine's propeller became a "runaway" and went completely out of control.

The disappointed team had no choice but to make an emergency landing at the nearest airfield, Sanford, Florida. No sooner had they arrived at their parking spot than the crew had to deal with a considerable fuel leak, which could be stopped only after the outer wing tank on the starboard side had been completely pumped out.

Perhaps Maurice Roundy would never have ventured on this ambitious project had he known how much work lay ahead. Almost ten years after her emergency landing at Sanford, the Starliner fanatic again ventured to restore construction number 1040 to airworthy condition. The "facelift" with a paint job that resembles the historic Lufthansa model was followed by an intensive overhaul of the airframe, supporting structure, engines, and systems. Roundy wanted to show it to all the doubters who ridiculed his lonely efforts at Sanford-Orlando Airport in Florida: at least this L-1649A was going to fly again! After twenty-one months of hard work, the moment seemed to have come on July 18, 2001. The third "maiden flight" in the long aircraft life of the L-1649A was imminent. The last landing-gear tests and checks of the four Curtiss-Wright R-3350-988TC18 EA-2 engines were successful at first. But at the last minute, fate struck in the form of irreparable damage to engine number 3. Of all things, this was the engine that was the only one not to have failed during the preceding flight. This was the end of the dream, but Roundy was not discouraged by this setback. His casual comment: "What do you expect from an engine that was last overhauled thirty years ago?"

After installing a replacement engine and months of further test runs, he scheduled the second takeoff attempt for October 19, 2001. After all final checks were positive the day before, the adventure could begin as planned. With Captain Frank Lang, the longtime chief pilot of MATS Connies at the controls, the Super Star lifted off from Sanford at 1:40 p.m. local time. Carlos Gomez, who along with Frank Lang had ferried the L-1049B originally purchased by the Swiss Super Constellation Flyers Association (SCFA) from Santo Domingo to Arizona, served as flight engineer.

During the flight to Polk City, all the Super Star's systems at first operated normally, until Carlos Gomez noticed the loss of all hydraulic fluid from the number 2 system. Captain Frank Lang immediately aborted the approach to the Fantasy of Flight Museum's grass runway, which was only 4,900 feet (1,500 m) long, and decided to land on the much-longer paved runway at Lakeland Airport. Once again, the project was on the back burner, since Maurice Roundy had put his last dime into this one flight to Polk City. But this time, luck was on his side. With their last ounce of strength, the two onboard mechanics managed to transfer the hydraulic residue from system number 1 to the second system by using a hand pump, thus extending the landing flaps. A landing in Polk City seemed possible again. Frank Lang set course again for the original destination. However, the adventurous flight by the former D-ALAN almost ended in disaster because the Super Star came dangerously close to a power line on final approach. It was only after a last-second overshoot and another circuit that the last flight by the L-1649A with the construction number 1040 ended after forty-five minutes on the grass runway of the Fantasy of Flight Museum.

After Lufthansa's failed attempts to return an L-1649A to regular flight operations with paying passengers, construction number 1038 now sits in TWA colors outside the TWA Hotel at John F. Kennedy Airport, while its sister aircraft, build number 1043, its components packed into hundreds of boxes, was transferred to Germany by sea transport.

CHAPTER 3 TWINKLING CONSTELLATION OF THE STARS

Wouldn't it be appropriate to name a constellation in honor of the Lockheed Constellation—the most elegant of all the magnificent silver birds from the golden age of aviation? Beginning with the Orion in 1930, the Lockheed Aircraft Company in Burbank, California, established a long-standing tradition of giving its aircraft designs an astronomically related name such as Vega, Lodestar, Sirius, Electra, Altair, or Galaxy. Below are some of Connie's most notable civilian customers around the globe. It is, however, far from complete—since a complete listing would be too extensive!

The passengers who flew on the Constellations were proud travelers. After all, it was still an expensive pleasure at the time to fly on an airplane, one that only a few very well-heeled people could afford. The luggage they carried therefore became showpieces of wanderlust and was adorned with labels of the airlines they flew with and the hotels in which they stayed. *Wolfgang Borgmann*

THE CARIBBEAN, CENTRAL AND SOUTH AMERICA

PANAIR DO BRASIL

Country: Brazil
Founded: October 1929
Constellation models operated: L-049, L-149
Unlike Cruzeiro and VARIG, which started with mainly German-born investors, aircraft, and expertise, Panair do Brasil did so with support from American sources. Originally founded as the New York, Rio, and Buenos Aires Line—NYRBA, on March 17, 1929, it created the operational conditions for regular air service from Miami along the east coast of South America to Buenos Aires—and from there across the Andes to Santiago de Chile. The main cargo carried was mail, for which NYRBA had acquired the lucrative licenses of the countries served, with the exception of the United States. On August 21, 1929, the airline's first Sikorsky S-38 flying boat took off from Buenos Aires for its maiden flight to Montevideo. Between February 19 and 25, 1930, the grand premiere followed from Buenos Aires to Miami. But NYRBA founder Ralph O'Neil had not counted on the charismatic and sometimes ruthless Pan Am founder Juan T. Trippe, who had already secured a commitment from the US Postal Service for the route. O'Neil's airline had thus become worthless, and he had no choice but to transfer NYRBA to Trippe, whose Pan American Airways was officially awarded the mail carrier contract by the US government just days later. On October 17, 1930, Trippe changed the name of his subsidiary NYRBA do Brasil to Panair do Brasil.

The airline put the first of three L-049s into service on March 31, 1946. That same year, one of these Connies, on a route-proving flight, became the first aircraft operated by a foreign airline to land at the then newly opened London Airport, now Heathrow Airport. In addition to L-049s, Panair operated L-149s before they were replaced on routes within South America by Caravelle VI-R jets with Rolls-Royce engines and thrust reversers. The airline took delivery of the four aircraft in 1962, and, after PP-PDU "Antao Leme da Silva" had to be retired as a result of structural damage, three of them flew in Panair do Brasil colors until the airline's surprising demise. In 1965, the Brazilian military government unceremoniously withdrew the airline's operating license due to alleged tax debts and transferred its long-haul routes and aircraft to VARIG, while Cruzeiro do Sul was awarded its South American routes.

VARIG

Country: Brazil
Founded: May 1927
Constellation models operated: L-1049E, L-1049G, L-1049H
Empresa de Viação Aérea Rio Grandense (VARIG) was founded on May 7, 1927, as Brazil's first airline and one of the first airlines in the world. Launched by German emigrant Otto Ernst Meyer, the airline took off with the maiden flight by the Dornier Do J "Wal" (Whale) flying boat "Atlantico" on January 27, 1927, from Rio de Janeiro to Porto Alegre, which was reached after two days. VARIG quickly established itself as Brazil's flagship airline with its reliable technology and good service. On the prestigious route to New York, VARIG initially used Lockheed Super Constellations in the 1950s, and from December 1959 its first S.E. 210 Caravelle I jets. Brazil's VARIG was the first South American airline to order L-1049G aircraft. In May 1955 the first of an initial three ordered arrived from Lockheed's Burbank plant at the Brazilian port city of Porto Alegre, which was an important airline base at the time. The sixty-six-seat Super Constellations were Brazil's first modern long-range aircraft. The commercial premiere flight by a Super Constellation under VARIG management took off from Rio de Janeiro on August 2, 1955, bound for New York.

VARIG also ordered two L-1649A Starliners in 1956 but converted the order to three L-1049Gs before the aircraft were delivered. With the takeover of the competing airline REAL in 1961, VARIG's fleet grew by four L-1049H models to a total of ten Super Constellations. VARIG did not retire the last aircraft of this type until 1966.

Panair do Brasil baggage label with a Constellation motif. *Author's collection*

Panair do Brasil L-049 PP-PDC on the ramp at Zurich Airport. *ETH Zurich*

A Varig L-1049G overflies the observatory on Mount Palomar, elevation 5,617 feet, located 50 miles northeast of San Diego. Two years later this aircraft, which was delivered to Varig in 1955, crashed off the coast of the Dominican Republic. *Lockheed Martin*

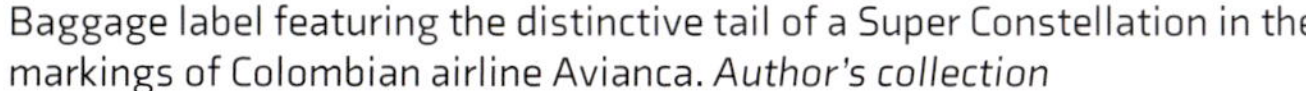
Baggage label featuring the distinctive tail of a Super Constellation in the markings of Colombian airline Avianca. *Author's collection*

Cubana also operated the L-049 and L-1049. This label promoted the L-1049G version. *Author's collection*

OTHER MAJOR CONSTELLATION OPERATORS

AVIANCA

Country: Colombia
Founded: December 1919
Constellation models operated: L-749A, L-1049E, L-1049G

CUBANA

Country: Cuba
Founded: October 1919
Constellation models operated: L-049, L-1049E/G

GUEST AEROVIAS MEXICO S.A.

Country: Mexico
Founded: October 1946
Constellation models operated: L-749, L-749A, L-1049G

LINEA AEROPOSTAL VENEZOLANA

Country: Venezuela
Founded: 1933
Constellation models operated: L-049, L-749, L-1049G, L-1049E

REAL

Country: Brazil
Founded: 1946
Constellation model operated: L-1049H

An L-049 of American Overseas Airlines at the Lockheed factory airfield in Burbank prior to delivery. *Lockheed Martin*

The L-049 with the registration NC90922 joins the AOA fleet in June 1946. *Lockheed Martin*

NORTH AMERICA

American Overseas Airlines
Country: United States
Founded: 1937
Constellation model operated: L-049

Founded in 1937 by the American shipping company American Export Lines, American Export Airlines (AEA) began using a Vought-Sikorsky VS 44A flying boat to connect the United States with Europe during World War II. On June 22, 1942, the aircraft, which had been christened "Excalibur," took off on its first scheduled flight from Foynes, Ireland, to New York's La Guardia Airport's seaplane station. In October 1944, a VS 44A operated by American Export Airlines set a new speed record of fourteen hours and seventeen minutes on the 4,960 km New York to Foynes route. AEA's flights were operated on behalf of the US Navy's Naval Air Transport Service, so most of the passengers during wartime were military personnel and diplomats. Immediately after the guns fell silent, AEA merged with the Atlantic Division of American Airlines to form American Overseas Airlines (AOA). It flew its Douglas DC-4s, Lockheed L-049 Constellations, and Boeing 377 Stratocruisers to Copenhagen, London, and Frankfurt, among other destinations. On September 25, 1950, AOA was merged into Pan American World Airways, which also integrated all seven of AOA's L-049s into its fleet.

EASTERN AIR LINES

Country: United States
Founded: 1927
Constellation models operated: L-049 (for publicity photos only), L-649, L-749, L-1049, L-1049C, L-1049E, L-1049G, L-1049H

Eastern Air Lines, once based in Miami in the state of Florida, put the first of fourteen L-649 Constellations it had ordered into service in June 1947. For each aircraft it had ordered one of the Speedpak freight panniers offered by Lockheed, which were loaded on the apron, raised by winches, and installed under the fuselages of the L-649s.

In addition to Model 649 aircraft, which were later converted to 749A standard, Eastern also acquired brand-new Model 749 aircraft and numerous variants of the L-1049 Super Constellation. These were used primarily on its low-cost air shuttle along the American East Coast. Eastern Air Lines was the first customer for the Super Constellation, taking delivery of its first aircraft from Lockheed in Burbank in November 1951. If Lockheed management had had its way, that role would have gone to Trans World Airlines. However, the disappearance of TWA owner Howard Hughes for months during the critical design phase of the L-1049 thwarted this. As a result, the basic version of the Super Connie was designed not as a comfortable aircraft for TWA's transcontinental routes across the United States and intercontinental long-haul routes, but as a spartanly equipped shuttle aircraft for Eastern Air Lines' short-haul routes.

PAN AMERICAN WORLD AIRWAYS (PAA)

Country: United States
Founded: October 1927
Constellation models operated: C-69 (for the US Army Air Force), L-049, L-749, L-749A

Along with Transcontinental & Western Air, Pan American was one of the first Constellation customers. In 1940–41, it ordered forty of the original version from the prewar days. The aircraft were supposed to be delivered in 1942, but the American entry into the war in 1941 thwarted these plans. In October 1945, PAA placed another order—this time for twenty-two L-049s—which gradually entered service on PAA's global route network beginning in January 1946. Initial Constellation routes were from New York to the Bermuda Islands, Portugal, Great Britain, and destinations on the African continent, as well as from San Francisco to Honolulu, Hawaii. In addition to the twenty-two aircraft ordered directly from Lockheed, PAA took delivery of seven additional L-049s from American Overseas Airlines

Eastern Air Lines was a major Lockheed customer that ordered almost every variant of the Connie, with the exception of the L-1649A. *Lockheed Martin*

Eastern ordered five different versions of the L-1049 alone. *Lockheed Martin*

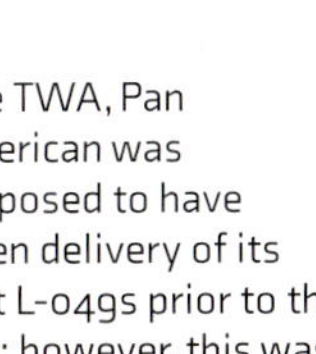

Like TWA, Pan American was supposed to have taken delivery of its first L-049s prior to the war; however, this was frustrated by America's entry into the Second World War. *Author's collection, Lockheed Martin*

Baggage labels like this one were distributed to passengers by Pan Am during the Constellation era. *Author's collection*

TWA ticket cover for a Constellation flight in 1946. *Author's collection*

This TWA baggage label was for a flight on one of its Connies. *Author's collection*

A TWA L-049 lands on the runway at Zurich Airport. *ETH Zurich*

TWA operated the L-1049, L-1049G (photo), and L-1049H models of the Super Constellation. *Lockheed Martin*

TWA launched its own series of decorative stamps with motifs of its destinations. *Author's collection*

This TWA postcard promoted a Constellation flight to Disneyland in Anaheim, near Los Angeles. *Author's collection*

This TWA postcard suggests a trip to Rome with the airline. *Author's collection*

The L-1049 is also the advertising motif of this TWA postcard. *Author's collection*

A TWA L-049 undergoes preflight preparations. *ETH Zurich*

Ramp scene at Basel-Mulhouse Airport. *Courtesy of Peter F. Peyer*

A typical TWA ramp scene in the early 1960s. By that time the first jet airliners had taken over the main routes, and the L-1049G no longer needed its wingtip long-range fuel tanks. *Jon Proctor*

External checks on a TWA L-049. *ETH Zurich*

A TWA L-1649A just prior to delivery at Burbank. *Lockheed Martin*

On the way to the ramp at Zurich. *ETH Zurich*

The former "Star of Switzerland" is now on display at the Pima Air and Space Museum in Arizona. *John Bezosky, collections and restoration manager, Pima Air and Space Museum*

after acquiring them in September 1950. Beginning in June 1947, five L-749s supplemented the Constellation fleet, which were sold to Air France as a complete package after only three years. By that time, Pan Am management's focus had turned to the Boeing 377 Stratocruiser, which took over the main air routes from the Lockheed propeller-driven airliners beginning in 1949. Pan American said goodbye to its last L-049 in February 1957, and there were to be no further orders for the larger L-1049 Super Constellation or even the L-1649A Starliner.

TRANS WORLD AIRLINES (TWA)

Country: United States
Founded: October 1930
Constellation models operated: C-69, L-049, L-649, L-749, L-749A, L-1049, L-1049G, L-1049H, L-1649A

The often-pivotal—occasionally tragic—role played by Howard Hughes as owner of TWA in the course of Constellation's development is detailed in various chapters of this book. From the perspective of TWA management, the airline was, for better or worse, tied to Lockheed through its major shareholder in the 1940s and 1950s. Nevertheless, with the exception of the L-749A and L-1049G, none of the Constellation models used by TWA met their expectations 100 percent.

As a result of the US entry into World War II, the company, still operating as Transcontinental & Western Air, was initially unable to take delivery of any of its Model 049s ordered in 1939. When the order for forty aircraft from prewar days was finally fulfilled by Lockheed in 1945, TWA had to make do with a spartan configuration that differed only slightly from that of a C-69 troop transport. It was not until competition from the much-better Douglas DC-6 in 1949 that Lockheed felt compelled to offer the L-749A, a Constellation model on a par with the Douglas model.

The eccentricities of Howard Hughes thwarted his TWA's involvement in the development of the L-1049 basic model in 1950—and it was not until the Super G Constellation of 1955 that all the demands made by TWA managers in terms of range, comfort, and speed could be met. When Lockheed offered an even-faster turboprop version, the L-1449, in 1954, TWA once again thought it had found a successful model for its own long-haul routes. But only days after signing the contract, Lockheed had to admit that the planned Pratt & Whitney turboprops were not available. The L-1649A offered as an alternative, with its four piston engines, was already considered obsolete technology at the time, and it met with little enthusiasm at TWA. The managers of Trans World Airlines were all the more relieved when Lockheed asked for the program to be discontinued and the contract terminated. However, both the manufacturer and the airline had made their calculations without Howard Hughes. He insisted on fulfilling the contract and producing the Starliner—to the horror of the TWA directors hoping to order faster jets, and to the delight of today's aviation enthusiasts, who can thus enjoy the sight of what is probably the most elegant Constellation model.

OTHER CONSTELLATION OPERATORS

Braniff International Airways
Country: United States
Founded: 1928
Constellation model operated: L-049

California Eastern Aviation
Country: United States
Founded: January 14, 1946
Constellation model operated: L-1049H

Capitol Airways
Country: United States
Founded: June 1946
Constellation models operated: L-749A, L-1049G, L-1049E, L-1049H

Delta Air Lines
Country: United States
Founded: June 1929 (start of airline operations)
Constellation models operated: L-049, L-649A, L-749A

Flying Tiger Line
Country: United States
Founded: June 1945
Constellation models operated: L-049, L-1049G, L-1049H

Northwest Orient Airlines
Country: United States
Founded: June 1945
Constellation model operated: L-1049G

Seaboard & Western Airlines
Country: United States
Founded: September 1946
Constellation models operated: L-1049D, L-1049E, L-1049H, L-1049G

Slick Airways
Country: United States
Founded: January 4, 1946
Constellation models operated: L-1049D, L-1049H

Trans Canada Air Lines
Country: Canada
Founded: 1937
Constellation models operated: L-1049C, L-1049E, L-1049G, L-1049H

Transocean Airlines
Country: United States
Founded: 1946
Constellation models operated: L-749A, L-1049H

Western Air Lines
Country: United States
Founded: 1925
Constellation model operated: L-749A

World Airways
Country: United States
Founded: 1948
Constellation models operated: L-1049H, L-1649A

An L-1049H of Seaboard & Western Airlines at New York's Idlewild International Airport, now John F. Kennedy Airport. *Allan van Wickler*

The ramp of the factory airfield in Burbank filled with aircraft awaiting delivery. In the second row is one of Seaboard & Western's L-1049s. *Lockheed Martin*

This TCA baggage label promoted a flight on one of the airline's Super Constellations. *Author's collection*

Just how nice a flight was in the L-1049's onboard lounge is suggested by this postcard issued by TCA. *Author's collection*

EUROPE

BOAC

Country: Great Britain
Founded: November 24, 1939
Constellation models operated: L-049, L-749, L-749A, L-1049D, L-1049E

Founded in 1939, the British state-owned airline for overseas connections put its first "real" land-based aircraft for long-haul routes into service in 1946 with the Lockheed L-049. BOAC also used the much-smaller Avro Lancastrian, Avro York, and Handley Page Halton, which had been further developed from World War II bombers into passenger aircraft but were regarded as unsuitable for passenger transport and offered very little in the way of travel comfort. The flying boats used by BOAC on routes to the British colonies in Africa and Asia after the war, whose base of operations was in Southampton in southern England, looked like dinosaurs from a different era of air travel.

On July 1, 1946, BOAC began a new chapter in its company history when the L-049 Constellation G-AHEJ, the first modern long-haul aircraft bearing the Speedbird livery, took off from London Airport for New York. Further North American connections, such as to Montreal and Baltimore, followed until BOAC acquired five L-749s from the Irish airline Aerlinte in May 1948, thus increasing the number of Constellations in service by 100 percent. These aircraft flew for BOAC primarily on its Asian route network and as far away as Australia.

After the airline's L-049 fleet was gradually replaced by Boeing 377 Stratocruisers on North American routes in the first quarter of 1950, it took over numerous other services to the Caribbean and Bermuda. The last L-049, with the registration G-ALCE, left the BOAC fleet in June 1955 after a Caribbean rotation that took it from London to New York to Trinidad to New York and back to London.

With the retirement of the L-049, BOAC leased in phases the four L-1049Ds built for Seaboard & Western specifically for the route to Bermuda. These cargo-passenger

The British government allowed BOAC to purchase Constellations despite tight foreign exchange, since no comparable British design was available. *Lockheed Martin*

A BOAC L-749A with the registration G-ANTF takes off from Zurich. *ETH Zurich*

An L-049 Constellation delivered to KLM in November 1946 is serviced at Amsterdam. *KLM*

The Constellation cut a particularly fine figure in the Flying Dutchman livery. *Lockheed Martin*

Ashtrays like this one with a model of a KLM Super Constellation were popular airline giveaways in the golden age of air travel. *Author's collection*

combos could carry up to eighty-six passengers in a BOAC-only tourist class. The last of these flights, marketed as the Bermudian, using the leased Super Constellations, took place in April 1956. The chapter of BOAC's own Lockheed L-749As ended in April 1962—sixteen years after the first flight by an L-049 bearing the Speedbird emblem symbolizing a bird in flight.

KLM

Country: Netherlands
Founded: 1919
Constellation models operated: L-049, L-749, L-749A, L-1049C, L-1049E, L-1049G, L-1049H

Founded in 1919, and thus the oldest airline in the world still flying under its original name, the Dutch airline relied primarily on Lockheed long-haul aircraft in the postwar years. Beginning with the first L-049s in 1946, the elegant propeller-driven airliners were used on the Flying Dutchman's

KLM took delivery of its first L-1049G in December 1955. The aircraft carried the registration PH-LKE. *Lockheed Martin*

Dutch washday on a KLM Super Constellation prior to its delivery to the Dutch airline. *Lockheed Martin*

transatlantic route network and as far away as its former Asian colony—today's Indonesia. After the last L-049 left the fleet in October 1950, KLM deployed L-749/749A and L-1049 Super Constellation of various versions in the mid-1950s, serving almost all of the airline's entire route network along with its Douglas DC-6Bs and DC-7Cs. Their era finally ended with the entry into service of the first KLM Douglas DC-8-32 long-range jets in 1960. The airline's growing fleet of jets gradually took over all overseas destinations from its proven propeller-driven airliners. KLM retired its last L-749A at the same time as the DC-8 debut in March 1960, while the last Super Constellation left the fleet at the end of 1962.

Lufthansa
Country: Germany
Founded: January 1953
Constellation models operated: L-1049G, L-1049H (leased), L-1649A

Baggage label depicting a Lufthansa L-1049G. *Author's collection*

This L-1049G swoops low over the boundary fence as it prepares to land from an acceptance flight prior to its delivery to Lufthansa. *Author's collection*

After its replacement by Boeing 707s and 720Bs, Lufthansa's L-1049Gs continued flying on European routes for several years without wingtip fuel tanks; for example, to Copenhagen, as seen here. *Tom Weihe*

Lufthansa's Super Connies wore this livery after their delivery in the mid-1950s. *Author's collection*

Mount Kilimanjaro seen from the cockpit of a Lufthansa Super G. *Didi Krauss*

Preflight checks on the central vertical stabilizer. *Lufthansa*

Sunset at the Lufthansa base in Hamburg. *Author's collection*

Singer Caterina Valente on the stairs prior to her flight on a Lufthansa Super Constellation. *Hamburg Airport*

Super G postcard with Constellation first flight stamp and a Lufthansa travel guide for Buenos Aires. *Author's collection*

Ticket holders in the 1950s were emblazoned with the flagship of the fleet. Author's collection

The L-1049G registered D-ALAP was flown by Lufthansa from 1956 until 1966. *Lufthansa*

A Super Connie from New York arrives at Hamburg Airport.
Author's collection

The Lockheed L-1049G and L-1649A were the first long-haul aircraft of the newly founded postwar airline Lufthansa. They were regarded as flying ambassadors of the still-young Federal Republic of Germany. On January 6, 1953—twenty-seven years to the day after the merger of Deutscher Aero Lloyd and Junkers Luftverkehr to form the original Luft Hansa—the Aktiengesellschaft für Luftverkehrsbedarf (Luftag) was founded with a share capital of six million deutsche marks. After the old Lufthansa had perished in the turmoil of the Second World War, Luftag's task was to prepare for the new start of flight operations after the end of the war—the approval of which by the Western Allies was still pending, however. The order for an initial four Convair CV-340s, four Lockheed L-1049 Super Constellations, and two Saab Safir training aircraft laid the foundation for Lufthansa's later fleet. The value of the eight-passenger aircraft, including spare parts, amounted to sixty-eight million deutsch marks, thus exceeding Luftag's share capital many times over. Financing was possible only through long-term installment payments to suppliers. Although the Douglas DC-6 was the first choice for a long-haul type from a technical point of view, Lufthansa opted for the less expensive Super Constellation for economic reasons.

Stuttgart was not a regular destination for Lufthansa L-1049Gs. *Stuttgart Airport*

This came as a great surprise to Lockheed—and to the amazement of the defeated Douglas factories. Even in August 1953, they could not believe the loss of the contract they had thought secure when Douglas submitted improved offers for the DC-6. But the decision in favor of the Super Connie was made almost overnight—and irrevocably.

After being renamed Deutsche Lufthansa Aktiengesellschaft, the airline took off on April 1, 1955. This had been preceded on March 1, 1955, by permission to import the four Super G Constellations. The first domestic flights were followed by the first European destinations from May 15, 1955—and transatlantic services to the United States from June 1, 1955. All the legal and organizational prerequisites for the launch of the new Deutsche Lufthansa AG were now finally in place. Ten years after the end of the Second World War, the new chapter in German air travel began.

WITH THE SUPER CONNIE ON LONG-HAUL ROUTES

The route network of the new Lufthansa grew rapidly from 8,069 to 53,545 miles (12,986 to 86,173 km) in its first five years. Even before delivery of the first of four Lockheed L-1049G Super Constellations, a follow-up order was placed with Lockheed on February 14, 1955, for four more aircraft of this type. The first aircraft, with the registration D-ALAK, was delivered to Lufthansa on March 29, 1955. According to historical company documents, it was the first Super Constellation ever to fly with wingtip fuel tanks. These torpedo-shaped auxiliary tanks at the wingtips could hold 580 gallons (2,200 liters) of aviation fuel each.

As the first flagship of the airline's fleet, Super Constellation D-ALAK was pictured on most Lufthansa publications intended for the public. The shock was all the greater when, of all aircraft, the D-ALAK crashed on approach to the airport of the Brazilian metropolis of Rio de Janeiro on January 11, 1959, with thirty-six of the thirty-nine people on board losing their lives.

The career of the L-1049G with the registration D-ALAP was also not without incident. On November 20, 1964, it made a belly landing with sixty-six passengers on board at Düsseldorf Airport. Fortunately, the accident was relatively minor. Although it returned to service a few weeks later, D-ALAP was the first of the seven remaining Lufthansa Super Constellations to be scrapped at Frankfurt on November 15, 1966.

On approach to the Egyptian capital of Cairo, this Lufthansa L-1049G passes the pyramids of Gizeh. *Lufthansa*

On June 9, 1955, the first Lufthansa Super Connie in scheduled service landed at New York's Idlewild Airport—today's John F. Kennedy. On board on a route test flight was Irish colonel Fitzmaurice. Together with Hermann Köhl, the night flight director of the old Lufthansa, and Baron von Hünefeld, the press officer of Norddeutscher Lloyd, he had crossed the North Atlantic in an east–west direction for the first time on April 12, 1938, in the single-engined Junkers W 33 "Bremen."

Seventeen years later, regular air traffic over the North Atlantic was already a matter of course. Following on from its pioneering role in opening air routes over the South Atlantic in prewar times, the new Lufthansa inaugurated a service from Hamburg to Rio de Janeiro on August 15, 1956. The commander of the Super Constellation with the registration D-ALEC was Lufthansa captain Rudolf Mayr. He was the first German copilot of the postwar Lufthansa and subsequently moved to the captain's left-hand seat. Mayr was no stranger to the route to Rio de Janeiro. In 1939, he piloted Lufthansa's last scheduled airmail service across the South Atlantic. With Baron von Buddenbrock, Atlantic flight director of the old Lufthansa, and the former airship captain von Schiller, other South Atlantic pioneers were on board Constellation D-ALEC as guests of honor on August 15, 1956.

On September 12, 1956, Lufthansa began service to the Orient—to Istanbul, Baghdad, and Tehran. These, too, had been destinations of the old Lufthansa. With the new routes, passenger volume increased by leaps and bounds. While it carried just 74,070 passengers in its first year of operation, Lufthansa counted 229,670 customers in the following year. In 1958, 622,487 passengers flew aboard Lufthansa propeller-driven aircraft, and in 1960, after entering the jet age, the million-passenger mark was exceeded for the first time.

In June 1955, Lufthansa was just about to introduce its Lockheed L-1049G on the North Atlantic when Lockheed Aircraft Corporation submitted its first quote for the purchase of the Super Constellation's successor. Four L-1649As composed the detailed offer, in which even the delivery dates of the Super Stars were scheduled two years in advance to the day. For a sum of USD $2.295 million per aircraft, the four propeller-driven airliners were to be handed over to Lufthansa beginning on October 31, 1957. The airline was given a cooling-off period of around four weeks, until

A luggage label bearing an image of an Air France Super Constellation. *Author's collection*

July 15, 1955, to decide for—or against—the offer. But Lufthansa did not allow itself to be put under time pressure, nor did it make the decision easily. It was not until March 1956 that the supervisory board gave its green light for the purchase—expressly against the recommendation of the airline's technical committee! The decisive factor in the vote "pro Super Star" was in particular its long range, and thus its ability to fly nonstop in both directions across the North Atlantic for the first time.

The first aircraft of the quartet, with the registration D-ALUB, was delivered to Lufthansa by Lockheed on September 27, 1957—almost a month ahead of schedule. The manufacturer hurried the delivery because the final assembly line for the L-1649A at Burbank needed to be closed as quickly as possible—and freed up for the new Lockheed L-188 Electra airliner. The next Lufthansa aircraft to follow was the L-1649A with registration D-ALAN on December 20, 1957. D-ALER was next on January 9, 1958, and finally D-ALOL on January 17, 1958. One month later, the Lockheed L-1649A production line came to an end with the delivery of one last Super Starliner to Air France—after just forty-four had been built. Lufthansa took six months to commission its new long-haul flagship. These six months were used for crew-training flights, equipping the cabin with—among other things—what was an ultramodern galley at the time, and eliminating technical "teething problems." And there were plenty of those. Even during the acceptance flights in Burbank by Lufthansa pilots, it became apparent that the crane airline's Starliners were not without their technical pitfalls. It was not until the third attempt and after a series of technical improvements by the manufacturer that the Lufthansa team signed the acceptance papers for D-ALAN and D-ALOL. D-ALER even required five test flights before Lufthansa was satisfied with the quality delivered by Lockheed. One of these acceptance flights was extremely dramatic, because a power recovery turbine (PRT) needed to increase the engine's performance failed in midflight. Fortunately, the crew was able to land the aircraft safely, but the Super Star was severely damaged in the incident. The ruptured PRT components not only affected the Curtiss-Wright engine but also perforated the Super Star's fuselage skin.

At the controls of Lufthansa's first Super Star ferry flight, from Burbank to Hamburg, was Lockheed chief pilot Carl P. Setili. The crew included Lockheed captain Paul Penrose, who was responsible for training Lufthansa pilots and flight engineers, and two flight engineers: Joe Rampoe and John Costa. Lockheed sent a team of three instructors to Lufthansa's technical base in Hamburg-Fuhlsbüttel to ensure that the technicians were also well prepared for the deployment of the new aircraft type. From October 2 to December 31, 1957, they trained the aircraft mechanics, avionics technicians, and engine specialists in propulsion and aircraft structure, hydraulic systems and flight controls, and air-conditioning and electrical systems. Lockheed also sent another five-person delivery team to advise Lufthansa on technical quality assurance, spare-parts management, and the preparation of service bulletins for the L-1649A, among other things. In addition to training, the Lockheed team also had to demonstrate its skills in troubleshooting, because the Super Stars

Constellation advertisement à la Air France. *Author's collection*

The Spanish airline Iberia also had a sizable fleet of Super Constellations. Its baggage labels featured a Spanish bullfighter motif. *Author's collection*

The L-049 in this photo joined the Air France fleet in 1946. *Lockheed Martin*

continued to cause problems after delivery. Among other things, fuel pumps proved faulty, leaks occurred at the emergency fuel dump valves, and the complex Bendix autopilot initially caused the technicians headaches.

On the day the D-ALUB was accepted, the first doubts were raised in Lufthansa management as to whether the concerns of the technical committee were justified—and whether the purchase of the L-1649A had really been a good decision, because a final weighing of the first Lufthansa Super Star revealed considerable excess weight. The planned nonstop route across the North Atlantic seemed to have become a waste of time with a full payload and adverse weather conditions. A comparison with the L-1649A previously delivered to Air France revealed that the empty weight of the Lufthansa aircraft, at 96,405 pounds (43,729 kilograms [kg]), was exactly 2,204 pounds (1 metric ton) above that of the French Super Starliner. Calculations were carried out feverishly, and every detail of equipment was weighed—right down to the 2.2-pound (1 kg) emergency ax. But all the calculations led to the same result: the Super Stars were too heavy because of the cabin equipment, which was tailor-made for Lufthansa. The weight problem had a particularly serious effect on a narrowly seated thrift class version, which Lufthansa had envisaged with ninety-nine seats. Lufthansa was therefore forced to plan a technical stopover for refueling on about half of all transatlantic flights between Europe and the United States.

An intensive exchange of letters ensued between Lufthansa and its aircraft supplier to bring about a quick resolution of the problem. The pragmatic solution was to increase the maximum permissible takeoff weight (without fuel) by 1,000 pounds (454 kg) to 116,999 pounds (53,070 kg). Lockheed also increased the maximum takeoff weight of the L-1649A from 158,700 to 160,000 pounds (71,985 to 72,575 kg). The higher weights required neither structural changes to the aircraft nor new test flights. Only the aircraft documentation had to be amended for the new weights.

The Frankfurt to New York route could now be covered nonstop even with a headwind of 60 mph (95 kph) to be expected over the North Atlantic in the winter months. At a cruising altitude of 15,000 feet (4,500 m), the maximum payload of the L-1649A would have had to be reduced by just 5.5 percent to 16,975 pounds (7.7 metric tons). Only when there was absolutely no wind, on the other hand, could the Super Star exploit its full-range potential, which amounted to a remarkable 4,722 miles (7,600 km) with a maximum payload of 18,078 pounds (8.2 metric tons).

Lufthansa celebrated the launch of its Super Stars on a grand scale. On February 13, 1958, a Lufthansa L-1649A took off for the first time in scheduled service from Hamburg—with a stopover in Frankfurt—on a 3,845-mile (6,189 km) nonstop flight to New York.

During the 1958–59 winter schedule, only two upgraded L-1649As, D-ALAN and D-ALUB, were initially available for flight operations. The first two Super Stars completed the required crew-training flights and allowed the launch of a once-weekly scheduled service between Germany and the United States. Beginning February 17, 1958, a Lufthansa L-1649A took off from Hamburg for New York every Monday. The two remaining Super Stars had not yet entered service in early 1958. D-ALER, delivered in January 1957, was still in the Hamburg maintenance facility, where it received its passenger cabin. On the other hand, Lufthansa canceled the aviation insurance on the D-ALOL aircraft for cost reasons, since it was not needed for the limited winter flight schedule.

It was not until the start of the summer flight schedule in 1958 that Lufthansa used its entire Super Star fleet for the first time. This permitted the replacement of the proven L-1049Gs on the prestigious New York route, which was henceforth served daily by L-1649As. Initially, the passenger cabins were equipped with a first class and a tourist class, to which a less expensive economy class was added in April 1958. From then on, L-1649A passengers could choose from fifteen tourist-class, fifty-nine economy-class, four first-class, and four deluxe-class seats.

Lufthansa's L-1049Gs, on the other hand, were in passenger service longer than the Super Stars. After they had supplemented the Vickers V814 Viscount fleet on European and domestic German routes with more-comfortable seating, Lufthansa equipped its seven Super Connies in an all-economy class with eighty-six seats for European and domestic German services by April 1963. A special chapter was the Air Bus service between Frankfurt and Hamburg. Originally, each route was to cost DM 60 less than a first-class ticket on the state railway. However, their concerns about their declining revenues led to the so-called Lufthansa Air Bus Service starting on April 1, 1963, with a uniform fare of seventy-five deutsch marks per route. Both Deutsche Bahn and Lufthansa were wholly state owned, and the German government did not want to encourage genuine competition at the expense of one of its companies.

Passengers purchased their Air Bus tickets from the purser on board the Super Constellation, there were no drinks or meals on board, and check-in at Frankfurt was in a very simple building, away from the other passenger flows. Lufthansa offered three flights each way on weekdays, and two services on weekends, which were relatively well received by travelers. After a first full year of Air Bus operation, Lufthansa and the Bundesbahn were able to agree on a reduction of the fare to seventy-two deutsch marks, but the Air Bus remained a relatively brief episode in Lufthansa's history.

From July 1964, Lufthansa withdrew its Super Constellations from European routes and limited its service to domestic German connections. The final flight of a Lufthansa L-1049G was by D-ALOF on a special flight from Copenhagen to Hamburg on October 6, 1967. There, all valuable components and the engines were removed, and four of the six remaining aircraft in service were scrapped. One of them, formerly registered D-ALIN, was initially used as an aircraft café at Hamburg Airport for several years until it was handed over to the Flugaustellung Junior aviation museum in Hermeskeil in 1980 and transported by flatbed truck to the Hunsrück region. A second Lufthansa L-1049G with the registration D-ALOP, which was exhibited as a flight café in the Hamburg district of Neu Wulmstorf, remained there as an attraction from 1967 until it was scrapped in 1975.

South African Airways relied on the four-engine L-749 for its long-range routes within the African continent and overseas. *THL Image Collection / SAR Publicity and Travel Department*

Built in 1954, this L-1049C was delivered to Air India International, which named it Empress of Nurjehan. *Lockheed Martin*

Air India operated the Super Connie versions L-1049C, L-1049E, L-1049G, L-1049H, and L-1049D. *Lockheed Martin*

OTHER MAJOR CONSTELLATION OPERATORS

Aerlinte Eireann Teoranta (Aer Lingus)
Country: Ireland
Founded: February 26, 1947
Constellation models operated: L-749, L-1049E, L-1049G, L-1049H

Air France
Country: France
Founded: August 1933
Constellation models operated: L-049, L-749, L-749A, L-1049C/G, L-1649A

Iberia
Country: Spain
Founded: April 1939
Constellation models operated: L-1049E, L-1049G

Sabena
Country: Belgium
Founded: 1923
Constellation model operated: L-1049H

Transportes Aereos Portugueses (TAP Air Portugal)
Country: Portugal
Founded: September 1944
Constellation models operated: L-1049G, L-1049H, L-1049E

AFRICA

Air Algérie
Country: Algeria
Founded: May 1953
Constellation model operated: L-749A

When the Société Algérienne de Construction Aéronautique, Air Algérie for short, was founded in 1947, what is now Algeria was still a colony of France. A number of L-749As were leased by Air France from 1955 for flights between Algiers and Paris. During the War of Independence, the first S.E. 210 Caravelle I, with the French registration F-OBNH, was delivered to Air Algérie on January 14, 1960, leading to the replacement of the Constellations on the Paris route. The L-749As were henceforth used to pick up secondary routes, primarily to destinations in France. The last aircraft was retired in January 1961.

Royal Air Maroc
Country: Kingdom of Morocco
Founded: 1953
Constellation models operated: L-749A, various L-1049s leased from Air France

Following independence from the colonial powers of France and Spain in 1956, Royal Air Maroc, or RAM for short, officially began operations the following year as the national airline of the Kingdom of Morocco, located in northwest Africa. L-749As, some leased from Air France and some purchased, replaced Douglas DC-4s on routes between Morocco and various European destinations. In addition, the airline also operated L-1049C and L-1049G aircraft leased from Air France. These were gradually replaced from

This historical luggage label was made in the shape of the continent of Australia. *Author's collection*

Qantas first flight letter from Sydney to Johannesburg on the Lockheed Constellation, and a photo of the first flight crew prior to takeoff on September 6, 1952. *Author's collection*

Like the aircraft operated by KLM, Qantas Super Constellations were given a symbolic washing (champagne) before delivery to the airline. *Lockheed Martin, QANTAS*

May 11, 1960, by Caravelle 1As, which were later converted to the Caravelle III version, and by three other aircraft delivered from the factory as Caravelle IIIs. Nevertheless, the last L-749A did not leave the Royal Air Maroc fleet until June 1970. Following the S.E. 210, RAM procured Boeing 707s for long-haul operations and Boeing 737s and 727s for use as short- and medium-haul jets and successors to the Caravelle.

Air Afrique
Country: France
Constellation models operated: L-749A, various L-1649A (leased from Air France)

South African Airways
Country: South Africa
Founded: 1934
Constellation model operated: L-749

Trek Airways
Country: South Africa
Founded: 1953
Constellation model operated: L-1649A

THE MIDDLE EAST, ASIA, AND THE INDIAN SUBCONTINENT

Air India International
Country: India
Founded: March 1948
Constellation models operated: L-749, L-749A, L-1049C, L-1049E, L-1049G, L-1049H, L-1049D

Air India was founded in 1932 by Jenhangir Ratanji Dadabhoy Tata as Tata Aviation Services in Bombay. It began operations with a de Havilland D.H.80 Puss Moth on October 15, 1932. In 1946, it became a public limited company and changed its name to Air India. Douglas DC-3s and Vickers Vikings were used on domestic routes, and Lockheed L-749s on the international network from April 1948 onward. Air India alone operated seven different Constellation and Super Constellation versions. The last Lockheed was not taken out of service until 1962.

Air Ceylon
Country: Ceylon
Founded: March 1948
Constellation models operated: L-749, L-749A, L-1049E, L-1049G

El Al Israeli Airlines
Country: Israel
Founded: November 1948
Constellation model operated: L-049

Thai Airways
Country: Thailand
Founded: 1951
Constellation model operated: L-1049G

AUSTRALIA

QANTAS Empire Airways
Country: Australia
Founded: November 1920
Constellation models operated: L-749, L-1049C, L-1049E, L-1049G, L-1049H

Founded in 1920, Australia's QANTAS initially used Lockheed L-749s from 1947 on the route it called the Kangaroo Route between Australia and Great Britain. Some of these aircraft were fitted with Lockheed's Speedpak external freight panniers to increase the Constellation's cargo capacity. On the route between the United Kingdom and its former crown colony, whose head of state is still the reigning British monarch, QANTAS cooperated closely with the British long-haul airline BOAC. The partners traded aircraft with each other—and crews from both airlines also flew each other's Constellations. On September 1, 1952, QANTAS expanded its intercontinental route network to include a connection to the South African metropolis of Johannesburg. The route, named after the wallaby, an Australian species from the kangaroo family, was also initially served by L-749s.

VH-EAB was a Lockheed L-749, which was capable of carrying an external freight pannier under the fuselage, as described in chapter 7, on air freight. *Lockheed Martin*

In 1951, QANTAS ordered its first L-1049C Super Constellations. This was followed by orders for the L-1049C, E, and H models—until an order for the ultimate long-haul version, the L-1049G, completed the airline's Lockheed fleet. The Australian airline did not part with its proven Constellations and Super Constellations until 1963—after sixteen successful and accident-free years of service.

CHAPTER 4
IN MILITARY SERVICE

CONSTELLATION

Beginning with the first production aircraft, the Constellation series was used in countless variants by the American armed forces. By the end of the Second World War, the US Army Air Force had officially taken delivery of fifteen C-69s—the first in October 1944 and the last in September 1945—but not all these Connies made it into service. The remaining orders were canceled by the summer of 1945. The main reason for this early retirement was the type's Wright Duplex Cyclone piston engines, which were prone to failure and, above all, caught fire easily, earning the Connie the dubious title of the world's most beautiful three-engine aircraft even in its early years. Thus, the USAAF and Navy opted for the Douglas C-54, which was comparable in its performance data but equipped with reliable Pratt & Whitney R-2000 Twin Wasp engines as their standard transport of the postwar period—with 1,162 delivered to the American armed forces.

It was with only ten examples of the further-developed C-121A/B military transport, based on the civilian L-749, that Lockheed succeeded in obtaining another order for its Constellation from the US military in February 1948. This order ensured the continuation of Connie production at Lockheed into 1949, which otherwise would have had to be completely discontinued for lack of other orders.

The C-121, which competed with the Douglas C-118, could accommodate a maximum of forty-four soldiers or, alternatively, military equipment loaded by way of a side passenger and cargo door. While the C-121A was rather spartan for troop transports and equipped only with the most-necessary comforts, with the VC-121A/B Lockheed produced not only the comfortably equipped first Air Force One presidential aircraft of the United States of America, but also the preferred means of transport for high-ranking American generals. The VC-121A, with serial number 48-610 and the name "Columbine II," was President Dwight D. Eisenhower's personal transport in 1953–54. On September 23, 1948, the US Navy ordered two PO-1W long-range reconnaissance aircraft, also based on the L-749, which were equipped with large radomes on the above and below the fuselage. The US Navy was so pleased with these two aircraft that it decided to order a fleet of WV-2s based on the Super Constellation, the last of which was not retired until June 1982.

The C-69 prototype was parked next to a Lockheed Vega 5 for publicity photographs. *Lockheed Martin*

This C-121A is now on display on Cheju Island in South Korea. *Lockheed Martin*

Flight deck of the C-121A. *Lockheed Martin*

The first L-749 destined for the US Air Force, with the military designation VC-121B. *Lockheed Martin*

The first airborne early-warning Constellation was the PO-1W, based on the short-fuselage L-749. It is seen here while on a test flight in September 1949 and was delivered to the US Navy soon afterward. *Lockheed Martin*

SUPER CONSTELLATION

After the military Constellation versions Lockheed C-69 and C-121, based on the civilian prototypes L-049 and L-749, the next generation of the legendary series was launched on October 13, 1950, in the form of the Lockheed L-1049 Super Constellation. As described above, the US Navy had already gained good experience with its two PO-1W reconnaissance aircraft based on the shorter L-749, which, together with the outbreak of the Korean War, led to an initial order for six PO-2W/WV-2 Warning Star Constellations on July 14, 1950. As long-range reconnaissance aircraft, the WV-2s were equipped with nearly 6 tons of heavy radar and electronics technology and were identifiable by their distinctive radomes installed above and below the aircraft's fuselage. Each of the aircraft had a crew of up to thirty-one and, thanks to two auxiliary fuel tanks in the fuselage and the two distinctive fuel tanks on their wingtips, could remain airborne for more than twenty-four hours without refueling. The certification flights of the radar-equipped Super Connie were again completed by Lockheed with the aged prototype, construction number 1961, which was equipped with dummies of the large antennas for aerodynamic tests. This aircraft was also used to complete the certification program for the Wright R3350-972-TC18-DA1 engines (military designation: R3350-34) that powered the WV-2.

Shortly after the first batch of WV-2s for the Navy, the US Air Force initially took over eleven Navy delivery positions on August 18, 1950, via R7O-1/R7V-1 transport aircraft based on the civilian L-1049B, designated C-121J by the Air Force and capable of transporting a maximum of 106 soldiers or military cargo long distances to theaters of operations. Military equipment entered the cabin through a large side cargo door. The US Air Force's first order for RC-121C Super Constellation radar reconnaissance aircraft came in January 1951, with the Navy's acquisition of an additional ten R7V-1 delivery positions. To supplement the RC-121Cs originally ordered, the Air Force first ordered the improved RC-121D version on January 9, 1952, whose structural design was the same as the civilian L-1049A model, and the first of which entered service on August 11, 1954. Among all the radar-equipped Connies, the WV-2E, equipped with a so-called rotodome, stood out. Its radar disk did not rotate, as is the case with the Boeing E-3A AWACS flying today for the NATO alliance, but it already showed great similarities to the current design.

In the 1950s, Lockheed placed great hope in the then-novel turboprop engine to make their military and civilian Constellation models faster and, compared to piston engines, more reliable. This resulted in the projected L-1249A, L-1449A, and L-1549A civilian versions. In 1953 and 1954, Lockheed produced the first two prototypes of the L-1249A turboprop Connie, which were offered to the US Navy under the military designation R7V-2 as a fast transport aircraft capable of carrying a maximum of 106 passengers or 36,000 pounds (16,329 kg) of cargo. The Connie's original wingspan of 123 feet (37.49 m) was shortened to 115 feet (35.1 m) for the L-1249A—and its cruise speed was increased from about 310 mph (500 kph) to a remarkable 440 mph (708 kph). The US Air Force also received two turboprops designated the YC-121F in 1955, which differed from the Navy's R7V-2s in having the conventional wing of the L-1049G instead of the latter's trapezoidal wings. However, neither the R7V-2 nor the YC-121F was ever built in series, since Pratt & Whitney eventually ceased further development and technical support for the PT-2/T-34 engine. Even an early-warning version called the W2V-1, based on the L-1649A Starliner, with a combined propulsion system consisting of four turboprops and two jet engines at the wingtips, never got beyond the drawing-board stage. Even the aged Connie and Super Connie prototype, with build number 1961, was used for various test series with turboprop engines from different manufacturers. The tests were primarily for testing future engines for the Lockheed C-130 Hercules and L-188 Electra. As a successful combination of an outstanding aircraft design and reliable turboprop engines, Lockheed sent the Elation (Electra-Constellation) to the starting line in July 1957. For it, the aircraft manufacturer's team equipped one of the two R7V-2 prototypes with four Allison 501 D13 turboprop engines, which later became standard equipment on the L-188. Certainly, the Elation would have been a viable option, but Lockheed had

Certified for a maximum of 106 passengers, the C-121C was equivalent to the civilian L-1049F. *Lockheed Martin*

A MATS C-121G photographed in flight. *Lockheed Martin*

The original US Navy WV-2 was converted into the NC-121K for electronic warfare in 1972. The last military use of this "Warning Star Constellation" ended in June 1982. *Lockheed Martin*

This page and opposite: The VC-121E "Columbine III" became the official presidential transport aircraft in 1954. It is now on display in the US Air Force Museum in Dayton, Ohio. *Lockheed Martin, US Air Force Museum*

Columbine III
26000
Columbine III

Just one example of this version, the WV-2E, was built. It had a radar dish with a diameter of 39 feet. *Lockheed Martin*

In 1955 the US Air Force received two YC-121Fs powered by four turboprop engines for flight tests. The aircraft's wings were identical to those of the L-1049G. *Lockheed Martin*

The Lockheed flight line on one day in 1953.
Lockheed Martin

opted exclusively for series production of the L-188, which was already underway.

The US Navy ordered eight WV-3s derived from the WV-2 on December 31, 1952, for service as "Hurricane Hunters." They were used by the Navy for weather observation and early detection of approaching storm fronts, replacing Lockheed P2V Neptunes. And yet another special military Super Connie joined the US Armed Forces on August 31, 1954, christened "Columbine III," President Eisenhower's second Lockheed transport. This Air Force–operated VC-121E was originally issued by Lockheed as the Navy R7V-1, and its rectangular windows in the style of a civilian Super Constellation visually distinguished it from all other aircraft of this type.

The aircraft, currently on display at the US Air Force Museum in Dayton, Ohio, is the only Lockheed VC-121E built. It served as President Eisenhower's personal aircraft from 1954 until he left office in January 1961. Eisenhower named this aircraft, his third Constellation, "Columbine III," after the official state flower of Colorado, in honor of his wife, Mamie. As the adopted daughter of that state, Mrs. Eisenhower officially christened "Columbine III" on November 24, 1954, with a bottle of Colorado water instead of the traditional bottle of champagne. Immediately thereafter, "Columbine III" carried the president, first lady, and British field marshal Viscount "Monty" Montgomery to Augusta, Georgia, over the Thanksgiving holiday for a five-day golf vacation.

The aircraft's most important mission took place in July 1955, when it flew Eisenhower and Secretary of State John Foster Dulles to Geneva, Switzerland, for the first peacetime summit between the leaders of the Western democracies and the Soviet Union. "Columbine III" served as the president's official aircraft for six years, and during this time it was also used by key US government officials and foreign dignitaries for high-priority flights.

After President Eisenhower left office, the US Air Force continued to use "Columbine III" as a VIP transport. The aircraft was retired from service in April 1966 and flown to the museum for permanent display.

Having so far diverted all its L-1049 transport aircraft from Navy orders, the US Air Force placed its first order for transport aircraft on December 16, 1953, in the form of thirty-three C-121Cs with higher maximum takeoff weights equivalent to the civilian L-1049F. The aircraft were used by the joint Air Force–Navy Military Air Transport

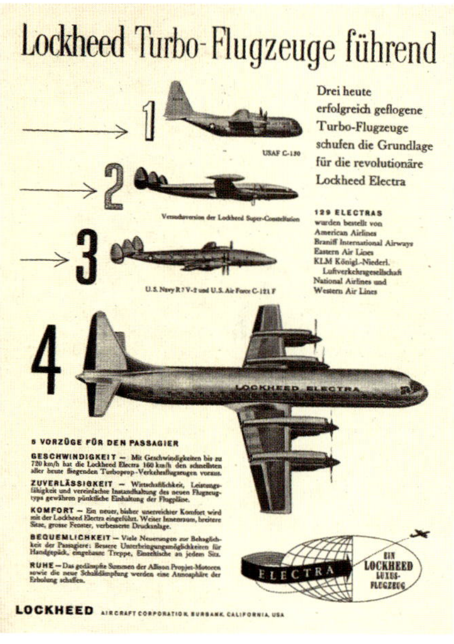

Lockheed advertisement in a German aviation magazine for the turboprop version of the Constellation and the L-188 Electra. *Author's collection*

The WV-2Es operated by the US Navy were based at the Naval Missile Center at Point Mugu in California. *Lockheed Martin*

Service (MATS) beginning on August 15, 1955. In addition to the US armed forces, Lockheed L-1049G and L-1049H Super Constellations converted from commercial aircraft to military transports were also used by the navy of India and the air forces of Indonesia and Pakistan.

Lockheed chief designer Clarence L. Kelly Johnson's passion for the Constellation design was shared by Lufthansa employees and passengers. As many as eight Lockheed L-1049G Super Constellations and four L-1649A Super Stars opened new global trade routes for West Germany from 1955 onward and, through the exchange of people and goods, gave wings not only to the economic miracle taking place in the young Federal Republic at that time. Their curved, dolphin-shaped fuselages, tall landing gear, and distinctive three-part tail, and the wingtip fuel tanks of the Super G Constellation, as well as the elongated, majestic wings of the Super Star, made them much-admired silver birds in the golden age of aviation. And like the royals in the flesh, the flying queens occasionally showed their capricious side, because their engines required a great deal of maintenance and frequently failed in flight. But such trifles cannot harm the reputation of a true queen. Quite the contrary—after all, numerous mementos from those days of air travel testify to the fact that Lufthansa was extremely proud of its first two long-haul types. Since the early days of the airline, no other aircraft types in Lufthansa's long corporate history have left such an emotional mark on employees and customers as the four-engine queens of the North Atlantic.

Lufthansa shared this affinity for its first long-haul aircraft with its customers in a variety of ways. These took the form of advertising posters, large-format photos, window displays, and travel agency models that advertised a trip aboard the Connies in Burbank, California, in Lufthansa sales agencies in prime city locations, or at the airline's check-in counters at the airports. Other advertising items included opulently designed brochures that presented all the advantages of the L-1049G and L-1649A to the traveling public, or ticket covers adorned with the unmistakable Constellation tail unit. Postcards showing Super Connies and Super Stars in action were also produced in small numbers and distributed exclusively to passengers during flights. This tradition was established in 1955, and unfortunately it fell victim to the red pencil at Lufthansa just a few years ago.

CHAPTER 5 MARKETING FOR A QUEEN

A MASTERPIECE OF CRAFTSMANSHIP

A uniquely beautiful piece that combines zeitgeist, craftsmanship, and love of the Connie in an incomparable way is a pocketknife shaped in the form of a Lockheed Constellation fuselage. This was manufactured by the Giesen & Forsthoff manufactory in Solingen at the end of the 1950s on behalf of Lufthansa. The so-called City of Blades is known the world over for its numerous metalworking companies, which have been producing mainly knives and cutlery since the fourteenth century. Then managing director Peter Giesen, together with Katharina Giesen, the fourth-generation owner of the family business, which has been in existence for a hundred years, described the complex manufacturing process that went into the Lufthansa knife, of which around a thousand examples were made, and this has been handed down in detail: "Its scales are stamped from brass, which is completely gold-plated in advance. The spring and blade are then inserted. All parts are then individually riveted with nickel silver pins. Finally, the two scales are laid out by hand in blue and the etching applied to the blade." That etching dates this knife to the late 1950s, since one side of the blade is adorned with the words

Lufthansa advertisement for the Super Constellation. *Lufthansa*

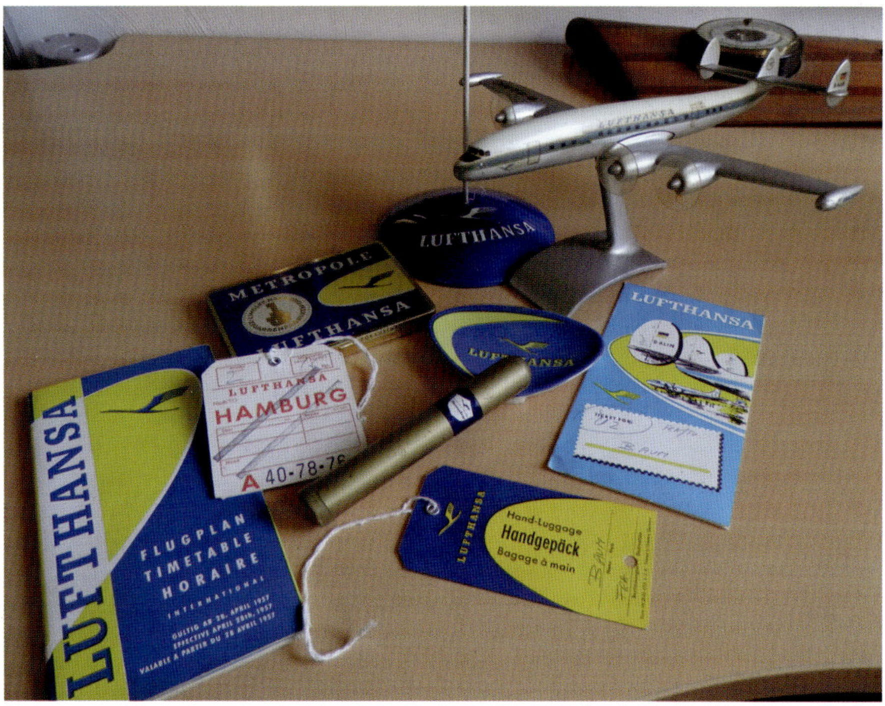

A Lufthansa Connie advertising collage, including a historical travel agency model. *Author's collection*

"LOCKHEED Super G CONSTELLATION," while the other side is marked "LOCKHEED Super * Star 1649A." Since the latter entered service on the Hamburg–Frankfurt/Main–New York route only on February 13, 1958, and was replaced by the Boeing 707-430 between the metropolis on the River Main and the "Big Apple" as early as March 17, 1960, the knife's production life can be reduced to this short period of Lufthansa history. An amusing allusion to the dolphin shape of the aircraft's fuselage, with a thoroughly practical use, can be found on its upper side. What looks like the fin of a dolphin is actually part of a bottle opener for removing crown caps that is recognizable only at second glance.

Lufthansa presented its fleet, including the L-1649A, in a small brochure. *Author's collection*

Historical travel office model of a Lufthansa Super Star. *Author's collection*

The same model can be seen in this photo, which was taken in the Lufthansa booking department in Dusseldorf in 1957. *Lufthansa*

Lufthansa folding brochure advertising the airline's Super G. *Author's collection*

When the Super Star became Lufthansa's flagship, the airline also produced a folding brochure for this type. *Author's collection*

From today's perspective, it is just as difficult to understand why pocketknives were given to passengers on airliners in the 1950s, and not only by Lufthansa, as why cigarette lighters were given out and smoking was permitted on board. Those were clearly different and, at least in terms of air travel, more-peaceful times. Since smoking was taken for granted around the globe at the time, and no one had yet thought of the health consequences, ashtrays designed in the then-popular kidney shape, matchbooks, cigarette boxes, cigar boxes, and cigar tubes formed from tin all bore the Lufthansa logo, as did cigarette lighters. Two objects designed with great attention to detail and highly coveted by collectors are the Snip lighters produced in the 1950s by Rowenta in Offenbach, near Frankfurt/Main, with the engraved silhouettes and type designations of the Lufthansa L-1049G and L-1649A. One side of each lighter is adorned with the Lufthansa logo in parabolic form, which was current at the time, while the opposite side presents one of each of the two Lockheed propeller-driven airliners.

The queens of the North Atlantic—to this day, the fascination felt by their fan base remains unbroken. Like no other commercial aircraft, their elegant design embodies the beauty of flight. And their surviving promotional items are silent witnesses to this passion, made of paper, plastic, and metal, carrying the flame of enthusiasm from generation to generation.

Like TWA, Lufthansa also distributed a set of small advertising postage stamps with motifs of the regions served by its Super Constellations. *Author's collection*

Pocket lighters were extremely popular promotional gifts in the 1950s, when comparatively more people smoked than today. Lufthansa commissioned Rowenta to engrave its two Lockheed long-haul aircraft. They were coveted collector's items then as now. *Author's collection*

Other smokers' souvenirs included small ashtrays in the kidney shape so popular at the time, as well as cigarillo tins and cigar tubes with the Lufthansa logo. *Authors collection*

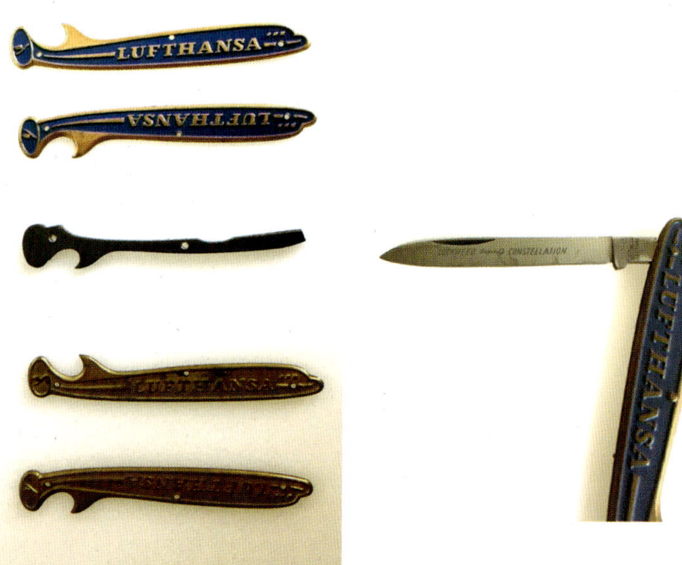

Lufthansa had small pocketknives in the shape of the Constellation, with suitably engraved blades made by a manufacturer in the West German city of Solingen, known for its high-quality knives, and distributed them on board its aircraft. *Author's collection*

CHAPTER 6
THE GOLDEN AGE OF THE CONSTELLATION

WHEN PASSENGERS WERE TREATED AS KINGS AND QUEENS

The Golden Age

"President," "Monarch," "Le Parisien," "Ambassador"—airline managers in the Constellation era were never at a loss for imaginative names for their opulent first-class products aboard the four-engined Lockheeds. The example of Lufthansa's "Senator" first class, which was first offered aboard the German airline's four L-1649As, illustrates the level of luxury that was common for passengers on many carriers around the globe in those "golden" days.

The Constellation flew in the so-called golden age, in which the customers were treated like kings and queens. This contemporaneous photo could not have expressed it better. *Lockheed Martin*

This arrival scene of a TWA Constellation could have come from a Hollywood film of the time. *Lockheed Martin*

The first discussions about such a service took place in March 1958 at Lufthansa's corporate headquarters in Cologne. Starting with the 1958–59 winter flight schedule, this "super service" announced by Lufthansa was to cause a sensation. It was to be "far above the level of the Lufthansa first class offered up to that time in terms of service and also in terms of in-flight catering." After just one month, a name for these very special deluxe flights seemed to have been found: "Golden Condor" was to be the name of the new service, which Lufthansa initially planned to establish once a week on the Hamburg–Frankfurt–New York route. In keeping with the title of this exclusive first-class service, the airline's remaining economy-class/tourist-class flights were to be marketed as Silver Condor service.

Lufthansa was not the only airline planning—or already operating—exclusive first-class flights between Europe and the United States. Air France, for example, operated a "Golden Parisian / Parisian Special" first-class service between Paris and New York. Pan American World Airways (PAA) offered private "Staterooms" aboard its transatlantic propeller-driven airliners, while Scandinavian Airlines System (SAS) offered "Royal Viking De Luxe" first-class flights to the USA on its Douglas propeller-driven airliners. What certainly hurt Lufthansa was the fact that SAS aircraft also stopped at the German airports of Hamburg and Bremen on the route between Scandinavia and the United States. If Lufthansa did not want to lose further market share in this luxury segment to the competition, it had to respond with an equivalent deluxe offer.

At an early stage in the preparations for the Golden Condor service, it became apparent that four beds would be offered in the rear of the cabin. An onboard lounge, a cozy meeting place for travelers above the clouds, was another highlight. Lockheed had already provided for the installation of lounges as an option in the fuselage section in front of the galley and had installed indirect cabin lighting at the factory. Lufthansa planners attached great importance to the fact that the aircraft of the pure first-class service could be quickly converted back into a mixed configuration with economy- and tourist-class seating to ensure optimum

Comfort on board a Lufthansa Super Constellation in the year 1958. *Lufthansa*

With the arrival of the Lockheed Super Star, Lufthansa introduced the particularly luxurious Senator first-class service between Frankfurt and New York. To this day a red rose is the symbol of Lufthansa first class. *Lufthansa*

use of the fleet. In July 1958, initial design planning began for the "Golden Condor look" of the Super Star cabin. However, Lufthansa designers quickly discarded the idea of installing gold trim above the cabin windows, or gold trim for the lighting fixtures on the ceiling of the center aisle. Likewise, the idea of installing small, removable Lufthansa signs in gold on the cabin sides was short lived.

In the middle of the month, the first doubts also arose as to whether the name "Golden Condor" had been a good choice. There were fears of plagiarism, since the American carrier Eastern Air Lines operated a Golden Falcon service. As an alternative, the name "Silver Star" was now brought into play internally as a possible name for the deluxe service. Regardless of this, preparations for the launch of the luxury service under the original name of Golden Condor service continued for the time being. By July 24, the details of an advertising campaign in leading American newspapers had been finalized. Even the cocktail parties to welcome the first flight to New York were already being planned. At the same time, Lufthansa was calculating the cost of every single promotional gift—right down to the matchbooks with Golden Condor imprinted on them. The design of the aircraft cabins, the uniforms of the onboard personnel, and even the naming of culinary specialties, such as "Chateaubriand à la Golden Condor," were also finalized.

Passengers on the Lufthansa deluxe service were to be given the option of membership in a "Golden Condor Club" on the basis of the number of miles they had flown or their social standing. Issuing passes, preferential treatment at airports, and complimentary hospitality at planned Golden Condor lounges in New York Idlewild, Frankfurt, Düsseldorf, and "other major stations," according to internal Lufthansa papers, were on the agenda. A tie clip would have identified male passengers as members of this exclusive circle.

In the midst of this far-advanced detail work, a letter from corporate headquarters burst in July 1958, calling the entire planning into question for cost reasons. However, Lufthansa's New York office, which had been heavily involved in preparations for the Golden Condor service, was not so easily defeated. On July 31, 1958, the New York Lufthansa employees wrote a letter to the Cologne headquarters in which they fought for the planned Golden Condor service with factual arguments. They declared the first-class-only service to be a strategic product to tap new, financially potent customer strata in North America. The large community of German expatriates in the United States, until then Lufthansa's most important customer base for North Atlantic travel, threatened to increasingly resort to cheaper charter flights for their frequent trips to the old homeland. These were offered by competitors at prices that Lufthansa could not match. Only a particularly exclusive product, according to Lufthansa's New York office, could stop this negative trend and bring new, affluent customers on board.

BIRTH OF THE SENATOR SERVICE

The arguments seemed to have borne fruit. On September 4, 1958, Lufthansa officially announced the start of the Senator service between the Federal Republic of Germany and the United States with the beginning of the 1958–59 winter flight schedule. At the same time, the Senator logo was presented as the emblem of the initially twice-weekly flights. What led to the abandonment of the name Golden Condor service has not been handed down. However, concerns about a possible accusation of plagiarism on the part of Eastern Airlines probably weighed heavily. On November 6, 1958, the first Senator all-first-class flight took off from Hamburg-Fuhlsbüttel with flight number LH 400. Before the leap across the Atlantic, additional guests joined the flight during stopovers at Frankfurt/Main and Düsseldorf. On Saturdays, LH 400 departed directly from Frankfurt and flew to New York with a stopover in Düsseldorf. In the opposite direction, the Super Star Senator departed Idlewild every Friday and Sunday at 4:00 p.m. local time and landed in Düsseldorf at 11:00 a.m. the following morning. After a forty-minute layover in the metropolis on the Rhine, the flight continued to Frankfurt. Every Sunday, the L-1649A Super Star took off from there again for the final leg to Hamburg-Fuhlsbüttel, arriving there at 2:30 p.m. On the other five weekly routes between Germany and the USA, Lufthansa operated the L-1649A in the mixed configuration with eighty-two seats.

A round-trip De Luxe–class ticket from Frankfurt to New York cost 3,957 deutsch marks at the time. That was roughly the price of a brand-new VW Beetle! For that, passengers also walked to the plane over a red carpet like VIPs and were welcomed on board with a red rose.

The Senator cabin of the L-1649A was equipped with eight seats in a forward first-class section, which was located directly behind the navigator's compartment. It was followed by the main cabin, with twenty deluxe seats, followed by the onboard lounge. The absence of overhead bins gave the lounge, dubbed a "club room" by Lufthansa, with its leather-covered walls, a "considerable spatial effect," as a contemporaneous Lufthansa paper noted. This was underscored by a special color scheme and indirect lighting. The lounge was followed by the galley, where a specially trained chef-steward prepared meals and drinks for the Senator service. He, along with three flight attendants, pampered Lufthansa passengers on long-haul routes. On board the Lockheed L-1049G and L-1649A propeller planes, good food and an extensive selection of beverages were part of good manners. The stewardesses and stewards therefore had to master the mixing of drinks, which was common at that time, as well as the perfect serving of the offered meals. The chef-steward, who prepared the meals for the first-class guests during the flight in cooking attire with a distinctive chef's hat, was responsible for their optimal preparation. The chef-stewards had no ordinary flight attendant training, did not necessarily have to speak several foreign languages like their colleagues in the cabin, and thus spent most of their time in their small galley, without any contact with the passengers. Their culinary repertoire included not only the à point preparation of fish and meat dishes, according to the individual wishes of the passengers. Rather, they also made breakfast dishes to order on a small stove, such as scrambled eggs or fried eggs with bacon. As the Lufthansa chroniclers note, it was considered a novelty in aviation history that these dishes served by the flying restaurant were prepared à la carte by a chef-steward for the first time. In addition to the white chef's clothing, his outfit included a personal chef-steward's bag. In addition

In the showcase of Lufthansa's New York City office in 1956, everything revolves around flight comfort aboard the Super Constellation. *Lufthansa*

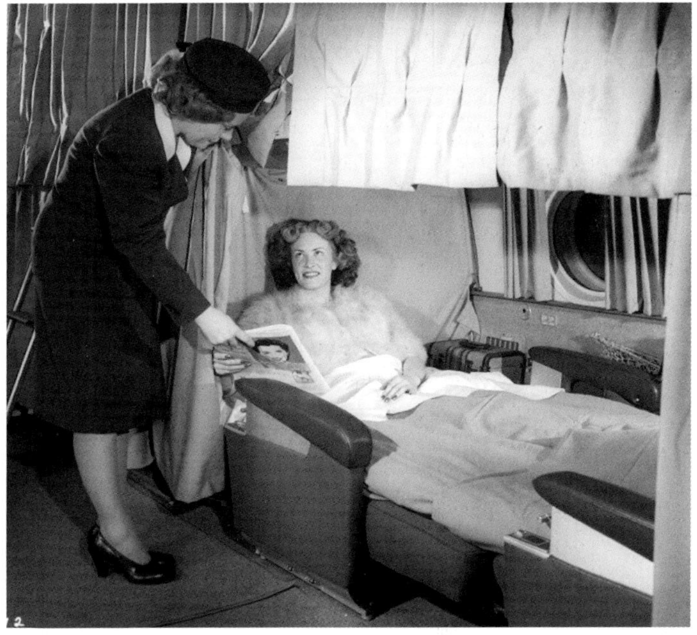

This cabin mockup shows how Lockheed imagined luxurious flight in its Constellations. *Lockheed Martin*

Traveling in elegance was part of the standard in those days. Short pants and flip-flops, common today, were frowned upon in the Connie age. *Lockheed Martin*

Along the way of TWA . . .

PARIS — ORLY

ORLY FIELD

Paris

From far-away places
across the world—
from New York, Detroit,
and Chicago,
from Rome, Cairo, and
Bombay—TWA's swift,
frequent flights
meet at Orly Field,
airport of Paris.

TWA
TRANS WORLD AIRLINES
U.S.A.·EUROPE
AFRICA·ASIA

This postcard distributed by TWA on its aircraft shows one of the airline's Constellations at Paris-Orly Airport. *Author's collection*

to spoons and forks, this also contained serving cutlery and valuable, extremely sharp carving knives. This bag was part of the crew luggage of each chef-steward and was always carried by him. A nightmare for today's airport security screeners!

The cabin crew would have had to save for a long time to pay for a flight on the Senator Super Star as full-fare passengers, because the Lufthansa flight attendants on board the L-1649A earned a mere 680 deutsch marks a month. Even with a so-called flight bonus, they didn't make more than 925 marks—which was about a quarter of the price of a single return ticket!

Toward the end of the 1950s, the era of the propeller-driven aircraft used in passenger service on the North Atlantic routes was slowly coming to an end. Despite their four high-powered turbocompound piston engines each producing 3,400 hp, Lufthansa's L-1649As flew a full 190 mph (300 kph) slower than the Boeing 707-120 jets used by Pan Am in direct competition on the North Atlantic from October 26, 1958. In order not to miss the connection to the jet age that was just beginning, Lufthansa signed a contract on January 23, 1957, for the initial purchase of four Boeing 707-430 "Jet Intercontinentals." Eight months before taking delivery of the first of four Lockheed L-1649A Super Stars on order, Lufthansa had already decided on their successor. After the first 707s began flying to New York on March 17, 1960, the Super Stars were quickly withdrawn from the main routes between Germany and the United States.

In this brochure, TWA illustrated all the seat variants in its aircraft. *Author's collection*

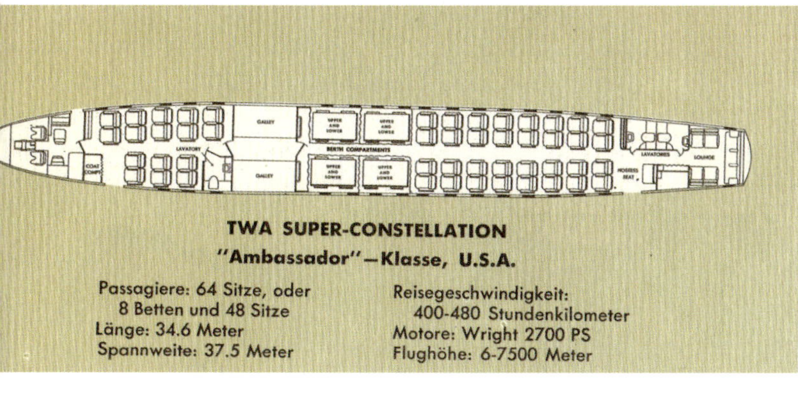

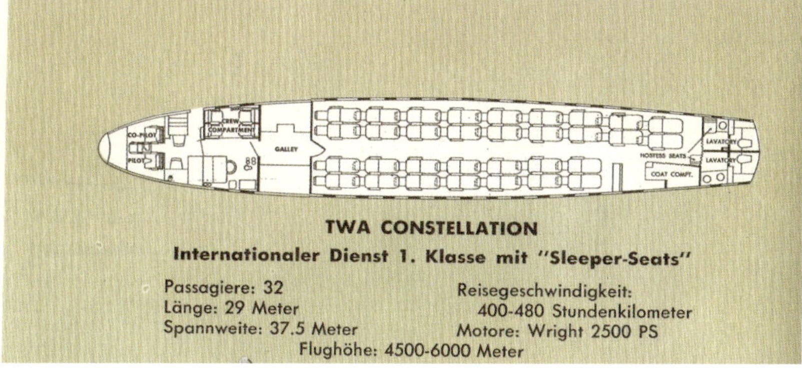

Comparison of the first class seating arrangements of a TWA Super Constellation, flying on US domestic routes (*left*), and a Constellation, operating international services. *Author's collection*

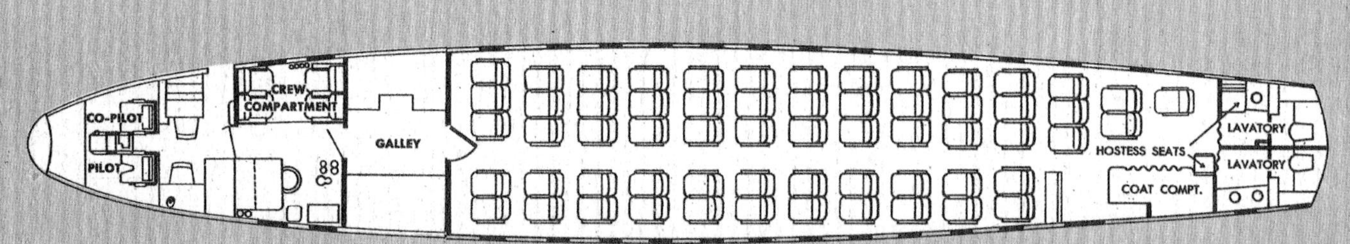

TWA CONSTELLATION

Internationaler Touristen-Dienst

Passagiere: 60
Länge: 29 Meter
Spannweite: 37.5 Meter
Reisegeschwindigkeit:
400-480 Stundenkilometer
Motore: Wright 2500 PS
Flughöhe: 4500-6000 Meter

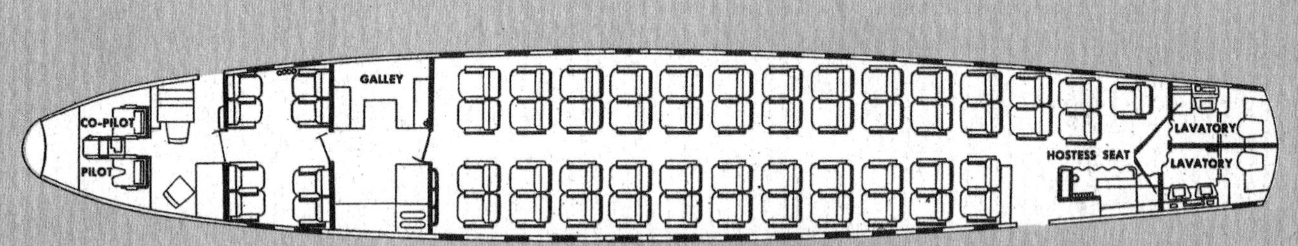

TWA CONSTELLATION

1. Klasse-Dienst in U.S.A.

Passagiere: 57
Länge: 29 Meter
Spannweite: 37.5 Meter
Reisegeschwindigkeit:
400-460 Stundenkilometer
Motore: Wright 2200 PS
Flughöhe: 4500-6000 Meter

The different seating configurations of the TWA Constellations. *Author's collection*

The popular Super Constellation onboard lounge was located in the aft fuselages of the aircraft flown by all airlines. Seen here is the lounge in a KLM Super Constellation. *Lockheed Martin*

Passenger check-in with Lufthansa at Frankfurt/Main. There were no security checks prior to departure at any airports at that time. They were definitely more-peaceful times. *Lufthansa*

As early as the 1950s, Lufthansa offered an escort service for children traveling alone. *Lufthansa*

Lufthansa stewardesses wore this uniform when the Super Constellation entered service. *Lufthansa*

LH 402

HAMBURG — NEW YORK

Februar 1958 February

HAMBURG — DÜSSELDORF
ABENDIMBISS SUPPER

DÜSSELDORF — PARIS
ABENDESSEN DINNER

PARIS — SHANNON
NACHTIMBISS MIDNIGHT SNACK

SHANNON — NEW YORK
FRÜHSTÜCK BREAKFAST
2. FRÜHSTÜCK 2nd BREAKFAST

ABENDESSEN	DINNER
Kleine Vorspeise	Small Hors d'oeuvre
*	*
Rinderfiletbraten »Excelsior« mit Wiesenchampignons und Hausmacher Spätzle Verschiedene Salate	Filet of beef "Excelsior" with Mushrooms Homemade noodles Assorted Salad
*	*
Obst	Fruit
*	*
Kaffee	Coffee

The menu from Super Constellation flight LH 402 from Hamburg to New York in February 1958. *Author's collection*

Right: The seats in the cabins of Lufthansa's Super Stars could be turned into comfortable beds. *Lufthansa*

Left: On Lufthansa long-haul flights, the cabin crew included a so-called cook-steward in professional clothing, who prepared fresh meals in the galley. *Lufthansa*

So-called berths folded out of the wall paneling on the Constellation and Super Constellation during night flights and could be converted into beds for a comfortable night's sleep. *Lockheed Martin*

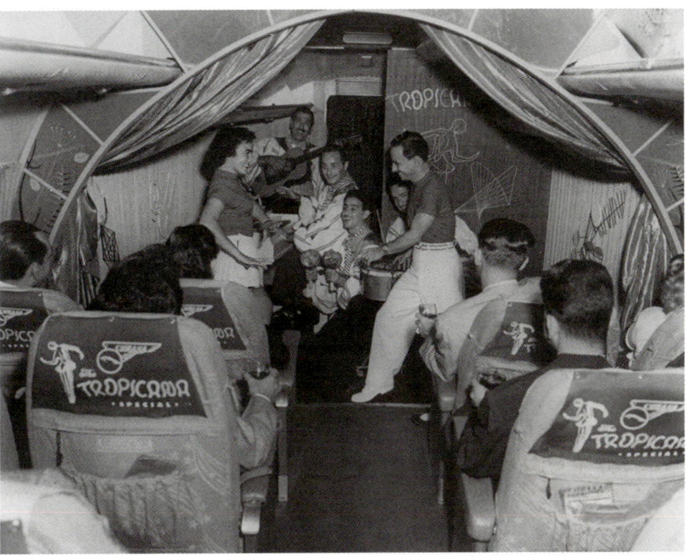

The passengers on Cubana's "Tropicana Special" were offered very special in-flight entertainment during their Constellation flights. *Lockheed Martin*

On board a L-749 in the 1950s. *THL Image Collection / SAR Publicity and Travel Department*

Traveling on one of South African Airways' Constellations was also a very comfortable experience. *THL Image Collection / SAR Publicity and Travel Department*

The SAA aircraft also featured a small lounge in the rear of the aircraft.

CHAPTER 7 THE CONNIE AS A MERCHANTMAN

CONSTELLATION FREIGHTERS GIVE WINGS TO THE AGE OF AIR FREIGHT

On September 19, 1783, the first "passengers" took to the skies in a man-made flying machine. The brothers Joseph-Michel and Jacques-Étienne Montgolfier had their hot-air balloon, known as the "Montgolfière," raised into the air from the courtyard of the Palace of Versailles before the eyes of the French royal couple Louis XVI and Marie Antoinette, where it remained in the sky for twelve minutes in front of the royal observers. For safety reasons, because they didn't quite trust the new technology yet, there were no humans on board, but a sheep, a rooster, and a duck. With a wink of the eye, this successful flight experiment can be described as the birth of air freight. Among logistics experts, however, the date of August 19, 1911, is undisputed as the historically documented birth of air freight itself. On that day, freshly printed copies of the daily newspaper *Berliner Morgenpost* were flown on board a "Harlan monoplane" from Berlin to Frankfurt an der Oder, a first. Company owner Wolfgang Harlan was originally a cab entrepreneur in Berlin when he joined forces with aircraft designer Karl Grulich to finance the production of the flying machine made of wood, fabric, and metal struts at Berlin-Johannisthal and to market it under his own name. And another premiere took place at the German capital's traditional airfield, when on February 5, 1919, the world's first regulated airmail service was launched from there with a biplane of the Deutsche Luft-Reederei between Berlin and Weimar.

All three events that took place in 1783, 1911, and 1919 are directly related to the Lockheed Constellation. This is because both live animals and, in particular, priority goods—who wants to read yesterday's newspaper?—as well as the transport of letters and parcels were among the highest-volume goods transported by Constellation freighters. Whenever speed, security, and reliability are required as part of a transport chain, air freight is usually the first choice.

The civilian Connies celebrated their premiere as freighters during the Second World War and during their significant participation in the Berlin Airlift of 1948–49, when they provided large-scale humanitarian aid by air to West Berlin, which had been sealed off by Soviet troops from June 23 to 24, 1948. They did not fly directly to Berlin

Under the fuselage of this QANTAS Constellation is a Speedpak freight pannier, which measured 33 feet, 4 inches in length; 7 feet wide; and 3 feet deep. It increased the Constellation's freight capacity by up to 8,200 pounds (3,700 kg). *Lockheed Martin*

but delivered supplies from the United States. Among others, the American airline American Overseas Airlines (AOA) flew its Lockheed L-049s between the United States and the West German airlift hub of Frankfurt Rhine/Main.

The Lockheed L-649 and L-749 were the only Constellation models that were capable of carrying a freight pannier under the fuselage. The pannier, called a Speedpak, could be moved on rollers on the ground and, if necessary, winched so close to the lower fuselage shell that it was flush with it. At 33 feet, 4 inches long; 7 feet wide; and 3 feet deep, the Speedpak increased the Constellation's freight capacity by up to 8,200 pounds (3,700 kg). Developed by Lockheed on the initiative of Eastern Air Lines, the freight pannier was very popular with L-749 and L-749A customers as the air freight business flourished in the 1950s. In addition to Eastern, the seventy-five Speedpak units produced were used by Air France, KLM, QANTAS, and TWA.

In addition to those aircraft delivered from the factory as freighters, Lockheed Aircraft Service Inc. (LASI) also offered the conversion of all models into freighters. The fact that this was worthwhile for the airlines is shown once again by the example of Lufthansa. As a result of Germany's export economy, which was growing by leaps and bounds during the "economic miracle," it transported more than 61,729 tons (56,000 metric tons) of paying freight just ten years later, after modest beginnings in 1955, the year it began operations, with a total of 606 tons (550 metric tons). This put the Crane in sixth place in a global comparison of airlines. On the lucrative and therefore fiercely contested North Atlantic, the airline even ranked fifth. Soon, the cargo capacity of the passenger aircraft was no longer sufficient to cope with the high demand. Therefore, in the winter of 1957, a Douglas C-54 (DC-4) freighter leased from Transocean Air Lines began shuttling between the Federal Republic of Germany and the United States. After two years, Lufthansa exchanged the C-54 for a Lockheed L-1049H Super Constellation freighter leased from Flying Tiger Line. In order to also fill the larger Super Connie on the New York route, a domestic feeder service was established with Lufthansa's own Douglas DC-3 freighters and a leased Curtiss C-46 Commando.

Loading freight into a Constellation at Johannesburg Airport. *THL Image Collection / SAR Publicity and Travel Department*

Parallel to the realization by the Lufthansa Executive Board that the days of the L-1649A in passenger service were numbered, the US Civil Aeronautics Board (CAB), which was responsible for approving flight routes to the United States, called on Lufthansa to use its own aircraft on its cargo flights to the United States and to terminate its contract for the L-1049H leased from the Flying Tiger Line. Thus, on Christmas Eve 1959, Lufthansa's supervisory board decided that two L-1649As in the fleet should be converted into freighters as soon as possible. Just one month later, Lufthansa and LASI agreed to convert two Super Stars, D-ALUB and D-ALAN, at a cost of DM 750,000 each. They were to be available for flight operations again by August 1960, and so Lufthansa applied to the CAB for an extension of the charter permit for the L-1049H leased from Flying Tiger Lines until the end of June of that year, which was granted to the airline. The new freighters, internally designated the Lufthansa L-1649FR, received two large cargo doors measuring 4.75 × 6 feet (1.45 × 1.83 m) (forward) and 8.85 × 6.17 feet (2.70 × 1.88 m) (aft). The maximum floor load was 299 pounds per square foot (1,460 kg per m^2). The pressurized cabin, lightened by the removal of baggage compartments, seats, kitchen, and forward lavatories, could now hold 4,767 cubic feet (135 m^3) of air

Ground crew prepare to load a variety of boxes of freight and packages onto the TWA L-049 Constellation "Star of Tripoli." *Dr. John Provan*

Advertising sticker promoting TWA's air cargo division. *Author's collection*

Seaboard & Western distributed these ashtrays with model Constellation to its best customers, in an effort to win their orders. *Author's collection*

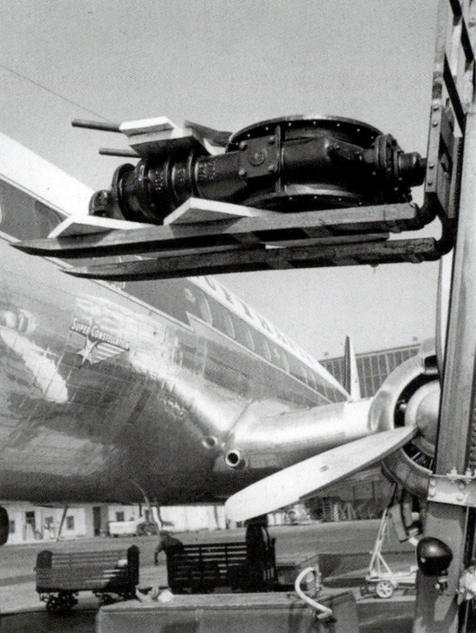

Even Lufthansa's Super Constellations, although not actually intended for transporting such large cargo items, were occasionally converted to freighters for special missions. *Lufthansa*

Production of Speedpak freight panniers and their use by Eastern Air Lines. *Lockheed Martin*

Advertising sticker for Pan American's air freight division. *Author's collection*

Loading equipment at airports was still fairly basic in the Connie era—as was air cargo in general, still in its infancy. *Dr. John Provan*

Lufthansa had two of its four L-1649As converted into freighters by Lockheed. One of the measures taken was the installation of a large cargo door in the aft fuselage. *Lockheed Martin*

In 1961 Lufthansa used this converted L-1649A to transport valuable breeding horses. *Lufthansa*

Porsches also traveled by air freight, though not on this L-1649A, following their new American owner's home. They had picked them up personally at the Porsche plant in Stuttgart, drove their new sports cars to Stuttgart Airport, and returned to the US aboard the Lufthansa Super Star. *Lufthansa*

Atmospheric night takeoff by a Constellation freighter operated by Catair. *Sjaak Roodenburg*

A Seaboard & Western freighter on the ramp at Stuttgart. *Stuttgart Airport*

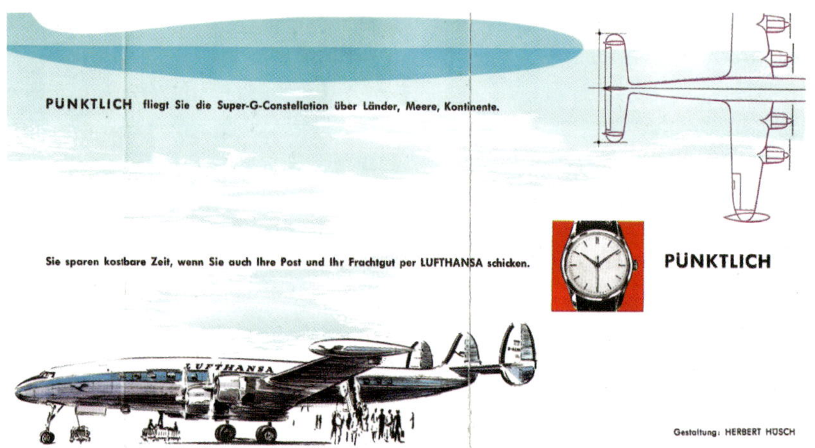

In this air freight advertisement, Lufthansa claimed that the shipments sent by its Super Constellations would arrive on time. *Author's collection*

Flying Tiger Line also gave ashtrays with model Constellations to its good customers and potential new ones. *Author's collection*

freight. In addition, there was 688 cubic feet (19.5 m^3) of cargo space in the underfloor. Lugs were fitted to the floor and sides of the former passenger cabin to allow cargo to be lashed down with ropes and nets.

The two L-1649A freighters D-ALUB and D-ALAN shuttled exclusively between Frankfurt/Main and New York. In those years, North Atlantic cargo traffic accounted for 30 percent of global airfreight volume, making it a lucrative traffic area. The breakthrough, however, came at the 1961 cargo conference of the member airlines of the International Air Transport Association (IATA). In view of the jet age, which had just begun, and the associated increase in efficiency, it decided to reduce the freight rates across the North Atlantic, which were binding for all members, by up to 65 percent. As if that were not enough, the rates were again massively reduced on April 1, 1964—thus further boosting demand. In addition to the greater capacity of the company's own freighters and the introduction of the first Boeing 707, 720B, and 727 jets, this was another reason why Lufthansa's annual freight volume increased almost fivefold between 1960 and 1966.

The following list describes the most-important versions of the Lockheed Constellation, starting with the prototype in 1943. It is beyond the scope of this book to present the countless military models, the listing of which alone could fill a book about the Constellation.

CHAPTER 8 SPECIFICATIONS

LOCKHEED C-69/L-049 CONSTELLATION

Manufacturer: Lockheed Aircraft Corp., Burbank, California, USA
First flight: January 9, 1943 (C-69 prototype)
Number produced: 88 (C-69 and L-049 combined)
Wingspan: 121 ft. (36.9 m)
Length: 93 ft., 9 in. (28.59 m)
Height: 23 ft., 5 in. (7.14 m)
Power plants: 4 × Wright GR-3350-35 Duplex Cyclones*
Cruise speed: ±285 mph (±460 kph)
Range: ±2,175 miles (max. payload)
Crew: 3 to 5 (flight deck) + 3 in the cabin

* The C-69's power plants. Starting in 1946 the L-049 was powered by R-3350-C18-BA-3 engines.

LOCKHEED L-749A CONSTELLATION

Manufacturer: Lockheed Aircraft Corp., Burbank, California, USA
First flight: October 1948 (converted L-749)
Certification: February 15, 1949
Wingspan: 121 ft. (36.9 m)
Length: 93 ft., 9 in. (28.59 m)
Height: 22 ft., 1 in. (6.75 m)
Power plants: 4 × Wright Cyclone R-3350-C18 BD-1
Cruise speed: ±292 mph (±470 kph)
Range: ±2,610 miles (max. payload)
Crew: 3 to 5 (flight deck, long-range) + 3 in the cabin

LOCKHEED L-1049 SUPER CONSTELLATION

Manufacturer: Lockheed Aircraft Corp., Burbank, California, USA
First flight: October 13, 1948 (converted L-749)
Number produced: 104 (L-1049G version)
Wingspan: 123 ft. (37.5 m)
Length: 113 ft., 6 in. (34.6 m)
Height: 24 ft., 7 in. (7.5 m)
Power plants: 4 × Curtiss-Wright 972 TC 18 DA-3 turbo-compound radial engines
Cruise speed: ±330 mph
Range: ±5,538 miles (0 wind, 0 payload)
Crew: 6 (flight deck, long-range) + 4 in the cabin
Note: specification for the L-1049G Lufthansa version

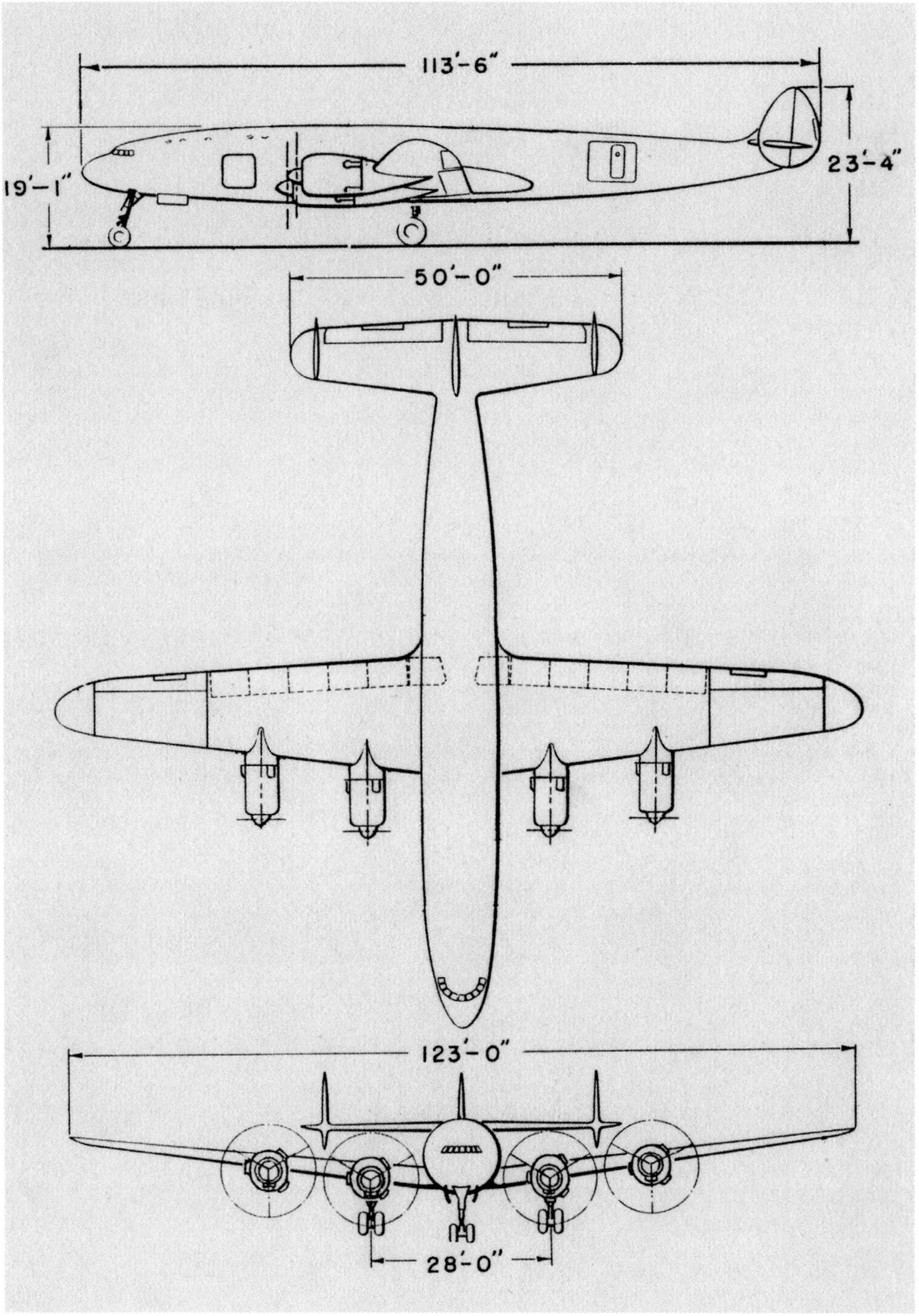

Three-view drawing of the Lockheed Super Constellation. *Lockheed Martin*

Copy
RM SL9H05a

NACA

RESEARCH MEMORANDUM

for the

Civil Aeronautics Administration

DITCHING TESTS OF A $\frac{1}{18}$-SCALE MODEL OF THE LOCKHEED CONSTELLATION AIRPLANE WITH SPEEDPAK ATTACHED

By Lloyd J. Fisher and William C. Thompson

Langley Aeronautical Laboratory
Langley Air Force Base, Va.

RM SL9H05a

NATIONAL ADVISORY COMMITTEE FOR AERONAUTICS
WASHINGTON

August 9, 1949

The dimensions of the L-749, including those of the Speedpak freight pannier, are part of this NACA brochure. *Ron Handgraaf*

LOCKHEED L-1649 STARLINER

Manufacturer: Lockheed Aircraft Corp., Burbank, California, USA
First flight: October 10, 1956
Number produced: 44
Wingspan: 150 ft. (45.72)
Length: 116 ft., 2 in. (35.42 m)
Height: 23 ft., 5 in. (7.16 m)
Power plants: 4 × Curtiss-Wright 988 TC 18 EA-2 turbo-compound radial engines
Cruise speed: ±342 mph
Range: ±7,021 miles (0 wind, 0 payload)
Crew: 6 (flight deck, long-range) + 4 in the cabin
Note: specification for the L-1649A-98-17 Lufthansa version

LOCKHEED L-1649A CUSTOMER NUMBERS AND EQUIPMENT VARIANTS

Lockheed prototype	L-1649A-98-01
TWA	L-1649A-98-09, -15, -16 (former Linee Aeree Italiene), -20, -22
Air France	L-1649A-98-11
Lufthansa	L-1649A-98-17

THE L-1049G AND THE L-1649A IN COMPARISON

Design Changes

Wings

- newly designed wings with large integral tanks for extreme long ranges
- prepared at the factory for retrofitting with turboprop engines
- thinner profile
- aspect ratio increased from 9.17 to 12
- greater wingspan (+ 26.9 ft.)
- greater wing area (+ 200 ft.^{2})

Power plants

- distance between engines and fuselage increased (4.9 ft. inboard and 6.9 ft. outboard)
- greater propeller reduction ratio leads to a 10 percent reduction in blade tip speed
- resulting noise reduction in cabin noise of 11.5 decibels, accompanied by reduced vibration level
- 150 hp increase in takeoff power thanks to new EA-2 turbocompound engines

Structure and technology

- new strengthened undercarriage
- wing skinning aft of the engine nacelles made of stainless steel
- added emergency exit in the aft cabin on starboard side
- two emergency exits over the wing on both sides of fuselage
- weather radar in nose
- more effective deicing system (rubber)
- reinforcement of seats and seat attachments for a load of 9 g

CHAPTER 9
THE COMPETITION

CANADAIR DC-4M / C-4 NORTH STAR

Manufacturer: Canadair Ltd., Cartierville, Quebec, Canada
First flight: July 15, 1946
Number produced: 71 (including the C-4 Argonaut and C-5 versions)
Wingspan: 118 ft., 1 in. (36 m)
Length: 93 ft., 10 in. (28.6 m)
Height: 27 ft., 10 in. (8.5 m)
Power plants: 4 × Rolls-Royce Merlin 624 or 724 C-1 (BOAC Argonaut)
Cruise speed: ±217 mph (±350 kph)
Range 3,045 miles (4,900 km)
Crew: 4 flight deck (long range) + 3 in the cabin

The Canadair C-4 Argonaut was a serious competitor for the Lockheed Constellation. *Author's collection*

THE CANADIAN DOUGLAS

The Canadair North Star was not only one of the most important postwar projects by the Canadian aviation industry, but also a very special milestone in aircraft construction. Canadair combined various aircraft components from another manufacturer with new engines and systems in the DC-4M to turn a good design into an even better one, a practice it would later use again to produce the CL-44.

The construction of this hybrid of a Douglas DC-4 and Douglas DC-6 with British Rolls-Royce Merlin engines was the result of a request from Trans Canada Air Lines (TCA). It was looking for a suitable aircraft to replace its proven Avro Lancastrian, which was, however, as a bomber converted into a transport, only partially suitable as a passenger aircraft. A TCA team therefore visited the major American aircraft manufacturers in 1943 in search of alternatives. Unfortunately, however, it was unable to find a commercial aircraft that would be available in the anticipated postwar period that would have met all the airline's expectations. Of all the models offered, including civilian versions of the Boeing B-29, Consolidated B-32, and C-74 Globemaster, the Douglas DC-4A and Lockheed L-049 Constellation came closest to meeting the Canadians' expectations. Detailed studies of estimated operating costs showed that only the four-engine Douglas DC-4A would be economical to operate on the TCA route network. In 1944, the Canadian government received approval from Douglas to have an aircraft built in Canada using components from the DC-4 and the DC-6, which up to that time existed only on paper. Engine selection was left to TCA, which planned to use its new airliner on Canadian domestic routes, routes to the United States, and transatlantic flights. A TCA document dated July 13, 1944, lists the piston engines reviewed for suitability: the Pratt & Whitney R-2000-9 and R-2800-C, Rolls-Royce Merlin and Griffon, and Bristol Hercules, as well as the Wright R-2600-22. Finally, after detailed analyses, all alternatives except the Pratt & Whitney R-2800-C radial and the Rolls-Royce Merlin in-line engine were eliminated. A final comparison finally tipped the scales in favor of the Rolls-Royce Merlin 620. The Merlin engine family was developed in the 1930s and was used to power numerous British aircraft types of World War II. These included the legendary Hurricane, Mosquito, Spitfire, and Lancaster. Built under license by Packard in the United States, the Merlin was also used in the North American P-51 Mustang. The Rolls-Royce engine was also installed in British transport and commercial aircraft such as the York and the Tudor. In contrast to the air-cooled radial engines in widespread use at that time, the Merlin was a liquid-cooled, twelve-cylinder, four-stroke engine. Its two cylinder blocks, each consisting of six cylinders, were arranged at a 60-degree angle in a V configuration.

Canadair Ltd. emerged toward the end of World War II from Canadian Vickers, which had ceased production when its major military contracts expired. The company initially stayed afloat by converting Douglas C-47 and C-54 military transports into civilian DC-3s and DC-4s for customers in North America and Europe, until its management learned of TCA's plans for a new commercial aircraft. Originally, the Canadian government intended to award construction of the DC-4/DC-6 hybrid to Boeing of Canada in Vancouver. But Canadair already had all the production facilities from the DC-4 (C-54) plant in Parkridge, Illinois, which it had acquired from Douglas. Included in this package were some seventy C-54 fuselages, which served as the basis for the first TCA aircraft without pressurized cabins. And so, Canadair in Cartierville near Montreal was awarded the contract for the development and production of what was to be known from then on as the DC-4M. Although it was initially "only" a conversion of existing aircraft, the development of the DC-4M1 presented major challenges not only for Canadair, but also for Douglas and TCA. Douglas supplied 30,000 design drawings to Canada from California alone, to which Canadair added thousands of its own designs. Cabin design was entirely in the hands of TCA, whose team first built a cabin mockup in which the various ideas were tested for their practicality. A Canadair team was also sent to Rolls-Royce in the UK to familiarize themselves with the Merlin engine.

At the beginning of 1946, the first aircraft, with the registration CF-TEN-X, slowly took shape on the final-assembly line. This DC-4M1 without pressurized cabin was actually intended for the Royal Canadian Air Force, but like five other examples of this version, it initially entered service with TCA on transatlantic flights. On July 15, 1946, the champagne corks were popping in Cartierville after the successful maiden flight of the aircraft, which was now christened the "North Star." Since Douglas feared that the North Star could compete with its own DC-6, Canadair was allowed to sell the DC-4M only in nations of the British Commonwealth of Nations. The buyers of this type were also contractually prohibited from reselling their aircraft to other airlines before the expiration of a period of two years or five thousand flight hours. This unusual clause alone shows that Canadair had obviously hit the jackpot with its DC-4M.

In May 1947, the North Star was first shown to a delegation from the British Overseas Airways Corporation (BOAC), which was looking for a modern aircraft for its long-haul operations. The Halton and Lancastrian, bombers converted into passenger aircraft, and the converted York troop transport were no more than interim solutions for BOAC. The Tudor, newly developed by Avro in Great Britain, had a disappointing performance and was not accepted by BOAC. Thus, in this case, the British government discarded its Buy British maxim and approved Buy Commonwealth in Canada as the second-best solution. On September 30, 1948, BOAC placed an order for twenty-two Canadair C-4s, which it would operate as the Argonaut. Like TCA's DC-4M2s and those of Canadian Pacific (CPA), BOAC's C-4s had the pressurized cabin of the Douglas DC-6.

The BOAC Argonaut with the registration G-ALHK and the name "Atalanta" became famous. Princess Elizabeth and the Duke of Edinburgh took off from London in her on January 31, 1952, on a planned round trip through the East African states. Elizabeth left England as princess and returned to Britain a few days later as queen of England aboard "Atalanta," following the death of her father, King George VI.

BOAC was delighted with their reliable Argonauts and operated their Douglas-Canadair twins until 1960. Most of these found new homes with smaller British airlines and the Danish charter airline Flying Enterprise. The last airworthy DC-4M North Star was retired as recently as 1975 by a small Florida-based cargo airline called Turks Air. A single surviving North Star is currently being restored by a group of volunteers at the Canadian Aviation Museum in Ottawa.

BOEING 377 STRATOCRUISER

Manufacturer: Boeing Aircraft Company, Seattle, Washington, USA
First flight: July 8, 1947
Number produced: 56
Wingspan 141 ft., 3 in. (43.05 m)
Length: 110 ft., 4 in. (33.63 m)
Height: 38 ft., 3 in. (11.66 m)
Power plants: 4 × Pratt & Whitney R-4360 Wasp Major radial engines
Cruise speed: ±342 mph (±550 kph)
Range: ±4,039 miles (±6,500 km)
Crew: 5 flight deck (long range) + 4 in the cabin

LUXURY ABOVE THE CLOUDS

With the Boeing Stratocruiser, in the late 1940s launch customer Pan American continued the glamour and luxury offered in the prewar years aboard the airline's legendary Clipper flying boats. On its two passenger decks, connected by a spiral staircase, the Boeing 377 offered everything that the discerning traveling public of the time expected. For example, there were separate dressing rooms and washrooms for each sex, as well as toilets. Five stewardesses and stewards looked after the maximum of forty-seven passengers, who were treated not only to seven-course menus in the president first-class service, but also to drinks in a cocktail bar on the lower deck, where the illustrious company gathered after the opulent meal. Horizontally folding reclining seats and real beds with mattresses, pillows, and comforters ensured a relaxed sleep even on long night flights. In the

The Boeing 377 Stratocruiser impressed with the luxury it offered on two decks, but it failed to score in terms of operating costs. *Boeing*

forward cabin area, it was also possible to rent two- and four-bed cabins aboard the PAA Stratocruiser, which offered maximum privacy.

An evolution of the Model 367, the Boeing 377 shared the final-assembly line in Seattle with the manufacturer's B-50 long-range bombers. The similarities between the two designs involved a number of structural elements and systems, including the vertical stabilizer and the Pratt & Whitney R-4360 Wasp Major engines. On top of the B-50's lower fuselage shell, Boeing placed the upper, wider passenger cabin, making the Stratocruiser fuselage look like an upside-down figure eight when viewed from the front.

Boeing produced a total of 888 Model 367 aircraft from 1944 to June 1956, which were used as C-97 transports under the Stratofreighter designation and as KC-97 Stratotankers for air-to-air refueling of military aircraft. Although the Boeing 377 looks very similar to its military sister on the outside, it differs from the Boeing 367 in various ways. Boeing invested about four million engineering hours in further developing it into a reliable and comfortable commercial airliner. The prototype took off on its maiden flight on July 8, 1947—a year later than originally planned. And another year and a half would pass before Pan American could take delivery of its first Boeing 377 on January 31, 1949. During the test phase, the Pratt & Whitney Wasp Major engines, which were prone to failure, were a particular source of concern. This problem was never completely solved by the engine manufacturer and led to various accidents and fatal crashes during the Stratocruiser's service life. The emergency ditching of Pan Am flight #6 after two of its four engines failed during the crossing of the Pacific on October 16, 1956, captured on film, became famous. After an exemplary water landing alongside a US Coast Guard vessel, all twenty-four passengers and seven crew members of the Pan Am Stratocruiser were rescued unharmed. Fifty-six Boeing 377s were produced, initially flying for American Overseas Airlines and BOAC in addition to Pan Am. Some Stratocruisers formed the basis for Aero Spacelines SGT-201 Super Guppy transports, which Airbus Industrie used to transport components between its European locations from the 1970s to the 1990s. However, not a single Boeing 377 has survived in its original form.

DOUGLAS DC-6B CLOUDMASTER

Manufacturer: Douglas Aircraft Co. Inc., Santa Monica, California, USA
First flight: February 10, 1951
Number produced: 286
Wingspan: 117 ft., 6 in. (35.81 m)
Length: 106 ft., 6 in. (32.46 m)
Height: 28 ft., 8 in. (8.74 m)
Power plants: 4 × Pratt & Whitney R-2800 CB-16 Double Wasp radial engines
Cruise speed: ±273 mph (±440 kph)
Range: 1,740 miles (2,800 km)
Crew: 5 flight deck (long range) + 2 to 3 in the cabin
Note: specification for Swissair version

ABOVE THE CLOUDS WITH A PRESSURIZED CABIN

With the DC-6 Cloudmaster, Douglas Aircraft Co. succeeded in building on the success of its legendary DC-3. Its predecessor, the DC-4, had been successful as a military transport, but after 1945, decommissioned military aircraft flooded the used-aircraft market and made the sale of brand-new DC-4s almost impossible. There was therefore an urgent need for a commercial breakthrough by a new type, which Douglas undoubtedly achieved, with 175 Douglas DC-6s and 286 more-powerful DC-6Bs sold.

The DC-6 resembled its predecessor—the DC-4—in numerous details. A heavily modified DC-4 (C-54) equipped with Pratt & Whitney R-2800-22W engines and with the US Air Force designation YC-112 served as the prototype for the civilian DC-6 as well as its military sister C-118. This YC-112 began the flight test program on February 15, 1946, making this date the official first flight date of the DC-6.

The DC-6 was very popular with airlines from the beginning, mainly because of its pressurized cabin, which gave the Cloudmaster a higher cruising altitude than its predecessor. On March 28, 1947, American Airlines and United Air Lines took delivery of their first aircraft at Santa Monica, California.

But the joy over the new additions to the fleet was short lived, after a United Air Lines DC-6 on a flight from Los Angeles to Chicago crashed in flames at Bryce Canyon in Utah, while a second American Airlines DC-6 burst into flames over New Mexico on November 11, 1947. Although the United accident ended in disaster, the American Airlines crew was able to make a smooth emergency landing. All occupants were able to leave the plane unharmed, and the flames were extinguished in time. Unlike in the first accident, investigators now had the opportunity to examine the wreckage in detail and determine the cause. In order to prevent further accidents, all Douglas DC-6s already delivered were grounded as a precautionary measure as early as November 12, 1947.

The Douglas DC-6 thus joins the list of famous aircraft types that are now aviation legends but were plagued by technical problems in their introductory years. Among these was the Lockheed Constellation, which, after several accidents in the summer of 1946, was grounded for six weeks until Lockheed engineers could identify and eliminate the sources of the problems.

In the case of the DC-6, accident investigators determined that fuel had flowed from the wing tanks into the passenger cabin heaters (due to a design flaw) and ignited. Douglas quickly scrambled to correct the fault, and by March 21, 1948, nearly a year after the first deliveries, DC-6s were back in the air. The accidents and subsequent grounding did not harm the popularity of the aircraft type, or the reputation of the Douglas factories. Perhaps this was also because flying was generally much less safe back then, and crashes were therefore more frequent compared to today.

Even while the DC-6 was grounded, Douglas was working on further developments of the type, designated DC-6A and DC-6B. Both variants had a stretched fuselage and a longer range compared to the basic version. Unlike the DC-6B, however, the DC-6A was designed exclusively for cargo transport. After their maiden flights, which took place on September 29, 1949 (DC-6A), and February 10, 1951 (DC-6B), the first freighters were delivered to Slick Airways and the first passenger aircraft to United Air Lines.

The Douglas DC-6 was a serious competitor for the Super Constellation and almost caused TWA to switch from Lockheed to Douglas. *Author's collection*

THE CLOUDMASTER ON POLAR ROUTES

After its initial problems, the Douglas DC-6 and its "big sister" the DC-6B developed into extremely reliable commercial aircraft. This prompted the Scandinavian airline SAS to offer flights on the shortest route between Europe and North America, over the polar region, for the first time with its brand-new Cloudmasters. On November 19, 1952, an SAS Douglas DC-6B took off on its delivery flight to Copenhagen for the first Arctic flight by a commercial airliner between the American West Coast and Europe. After taking off from Los Angeles, the SAS crew made refueling stops at Edmonton in Canada and Thule, Greenland. Further tests followed on subsequent delivery flights of brand-new Douglas DC-6Bs to Denmark. One of these was the first flight with passengers and mail on December 5–6, 1952. By 1954, the SAS pioneers finally felt secure enough to inaugurate the first scheduled commercial service over the Arctic. On November 15 of that year, the DC-6B "Helge Viking" took off on a flight from Copenhagen to Los Angeles amid a flurry of flashbulbs from the world's press. For five years, SAS remained unrivaled with this fastest connection between California and Europe!

DOUGLAS DC-7C SEVEN SEAS

Manufacturer: Douglas Aircraft Co. Inc., Santa Monica, California, USA
First flight: May 18, 1953
Number produced: 338
Wingspan: 127 ft., 6 in. (38.86 m)
Length: 113 ft., 6 in. (34.58 m)
Height: 30 ft., 9 in. (9.37 m)
Power plants: 4 × Wright R-3350 turbocompound radial engines
Cruise speed: ±341 mph (±550 kph)
Range: 4,008 miles (6,450 km)
Crew: 5 flight deck (long range) + 3 to 4 in the cabin
Note: specification for Swissair version of the DC-7C

THE LAST DOUGLAS PROPELLER-DRIVEN AIRLINER

The Douglas DC-7C was at the end of a long evolutionary chain of successful propeller-driven airliners produced by Douglas. The impetus for the development of the DC-7 came from the president of American Airlines, C. R. Smith. He had already convinced Douglas to build the DC-3 in 1934, thus laying the foundation for the success story of the aircraft manufacturer based in Santa Monica, California. Smith now demanded a further development of the DC-6B, which Douglas sent out on its maiden flight on May 18, 1953, in the form of the DC-7. On November 4, 1953, an aircraft of this type entered service for the first time with American Airlines, which now offered nonstop flights between the American East and West Coasts.

Eastern Airlines initiated the DC-7B, which first flew on April 21, 1955, and had a range some 560 miles (900 km) greater than the DC-7. It was followed by the ultimate DC-7C Seven Seas long-range version. The first customer, Pan Am, put the first aircraft of this type into service on April 18, 1956, serving destinations mainly on its extensive route network in the Pacific. The DC-7C was thus available about a year earlier than the Lockheed L-1649A Starliner, its direct competitor. The DC-7C was also used by numerous airlines in Europe. Among them were BOAC, KLM, Swissair, and the Scandinavian airline SAS.

However, the impressive performance data of the last great Douglas propeller-driven airliner could not hide the fact that the era of piston-engined aircraft on long-haul routes was coming to an end with the dawn of the jet age. Less than two years after the DC-7C's first flight, BOAC inaugurated commercial jet air service over the North Atlantic with a de Havilland D.H. 106 Comet 4 on October 4, 1958. Pan Am followed just a few days later, on October 26 of that year, with the Boeing 707-120 Clipper America. Passengers traveling aboard the new jets were not quite as comfortable as they had been in the days of propeller-driven aircraft, but they were almost twice as fast and much quieter. The almost vibration-free Rolls-Royce Avon and Pratt & Whitney JT3 jet engines of the two jet pioneers were a boon to passengers compared to the piston engines of the classic propliners with their vibration and noise. In addition, the new jets flew much higher, far above the turbulence zones in which the propeller planes usually traveled.

The Douglas 7C was a direct contender to the Lockheed L-1649A. Although more successful than the Lockheed. *Tom Weihe*

BIBLIOGRAPHY

Davies, R. E. G. *Pan AM: An Airline and Its Aircraft.* Twickenham, UK: Hamlyn, 1987.

Marson, Peter J. *The Lockheed Constellation.* Tonbridge, UK: Air-Britain, 2007.

Contemporaneous documents, Lufthansa.

Contemporaneous documents, BOAC.

Contemporaneous documents, Pan Am.

Contemporaneous documents, TWA.

ACKNOWLEDGMENTS

Numerous individuals and organizations contributed to the success of this book. In particular, I would like to thank John Bezosky, collections manager, Pima Air and Space Museum, USA; Dave Robinson, www.aviationancestry.co.uk, Great Britain; and Tom Weihe and Musante Larsen, Nicolai, Denmark; as well as my dear wife, Carol Oxberry, for her continued support through advice, action, and patience in the creation of this book!

THE AUTHOR
WOLFGANG BORGMANN

Wolfgang Borgmann's enthusiasm for aviation was passed on to him by his parents, who were active in the aviation field. In his early years, he began building up an aviation historical collection that provides numerous rare photos and documents, as well as exciting background information, for his books. Since April 2000, Borgmann has been active as an author and freelance aviation journalist. He lives in Bielefeld, Germany. His website is www.aerojournalist.de.